A LAMP
UNTO
YOURSELF

A LAMP UNTO YOURSELF

A BEGINNER'S GUIDE TO
ASIAN SPIRITUAL PRACTICES,
FROM ADVAITA AND BUDDHISM
TO YOGA AND ZEN

C. PIERCE SALGUERO, PHD

BEACON PRESS, BOSTON

BEACON PRESS
Boston, Massachusetts
www.beacon.org

Beacon Press books
are published under the auspices of
the Unitarian Universalist Association of Congregations.

28 27 26 25   8 7 6 5 4 3 2 1

This book is printed on acid-free paper that meets the uncoated paper
ANSI/NISO specifications for permanence as revised in 1992.

Text design and composition by Kim Arney

Library of Congress Cataloging-in-Publication Data
Names: Salguero, C. Pierce, author.
Title: A lamp unto yourself : a beginner's guide to Asian spiritual practices,
from Advaita and Buddhism to yoga and zen / C. Pierce Salguero, PhD.
Description: Boston : Beacon Press, [2025] |
Summary: "For "spiritual explorers" ready to travel beyond Western
bounds, a beginner's guide to Asian spiritual traditions spanning regions,
cultures, and history" —Provided by publisher.
Identifiers: LCCN 2024050662 (print) | LCCN 2024050663 (ebook) |
ISBN 9780807020395 (hardcover) | ISBN 9780807020388 (ebook)
Subjects: LCSH: Spirituality—Asia. | Spiritual life—Buddhism. | Spiritual
life—Hinduism. | Spiritual life—Taoism. | Spiritual life—Zen Buddhism.
Classification: LCC BQ9288 .S254 2025 (print) | LCC BQ9288 (ebook) |
DDC 294.3/444—c23/eng/20250110
LC record available at https://lccn.loc.gov/2024050662
LC ebook record available at https://lccn.loc.gov/2024050663

To all spiritual seekers:

may your lamp shine brightly,
illuminating the path before you
as you step into the mystery.

CONTENTS

PREFACE

Ancient writings from India preserve a story about the death of one of the most influential spiritual masters of all time. This narrative was carried orally for centuries until it was written down in the first century BCE in an Indian language called Pali, in a scripture named *The Discourse About the Great Emancipation* (*Maha-parinibbana Sutta*). The text details the teachings, miracles, and other activities the Buddha performed in his final days.

The Buddha had spent over four decades, from the time of his enlightenment at the age of thirty-five to the time of his death at eighty, expounding his teachings to thousands of people. Yet, even as his illness was becoming progressively worse and his body was beginning to fail, his faithful attendant Ananda asked the Buddha for some final words of wisdom.

The Buddha replied that he had never held back anything from his disciples and had no final secret teaching to reveal. As he would soon no longer be there to provide guidance, he exhorted Ananda to stop relying on him for all the answers. "Be a lamp unto yourself," he said, "a refuge unto yourself."* The master had laid out all of the teachings with clarity and precision; it was now up to each student to take up the initiative to put them into practice.

---

*As is often the case with terms in ancient texts, there is some ambiguity about the Pali word *dipa*. I am following the Chinese tradition, popular among many Western translators as well, to translate this term as "lamp" or "light." The alternative meaning is "island," and in my opinion, "be an island unto yourself" works just as well.

This simple phrase has been deeply inspirational for many modern spiritual seekers. It evokes a radically different ethos than we normally expect from religious leaders, doesn't it? The Buddha's message is not that you should take refuge in scriptures, gods, institutions, or charismatic gurus. He does not ask you to place your faith in anything other than your own discrimination and due diligence. He had shared his own discoveries in as much detail as he could, but each of us has to experience the truth for ourselves.

Those qualities of self-reliance, autonomy, and firsthand experience are features of what I call "spiritual exploration," and that's what this book is about. Simply put, spiritual exploration is about empowering you rather than indoctrinating you. There are plenty of other books out there that will mold you into a faithful Buddhist, a good Hindu, a proper Taoist, or a serious yogi. Here, in contrast, we will be investigating what the practice of Asian spiritual traditions can offer us while always maintaining a noncommitted stance. We will treat the entire range of Asian spiritual ideas and practices as a menu of options that all have their own advantages and disadvantages, and that may or may not resonate with different people. You will make up your own mind about what works for you.

There are some concerns and potential pitfalls with this kind of piecemeal approach. You might wonder if it's even possible to practice ancient traditions when living in the hypermodern contemporary world. How can we be sure about the accuracy of our understanding as we learn about new traditions? What about cultural appropriation and other ethical issues? These thorny questions are immensely important, and I talk about them in detail in the final chapter of the book. (If these concerns feel especially urgent or are preventing you from enjoying reading, then by all means please feel free to skip ahead and read that chapter first.)

Despite these potential snags, however, my argument in this book is that it is entirely possible to customize a blend of practices that can be personally meaningful and truly transformative, while also being a good fit for your life and your own priorities. If that sounds like an approach you would be interested in, then you are most welcome to join me on this journey of exploration!

What's the point of this journey? Perhaps you, like most spiritual explorers, are seeking something deeper, more fulfilling, more alive, more soulful than where you are now. In my experience, the vast majority of people who get interested in this topic are primarily seeking health and wholeness. Many are driven to start this journey because they are either suffering due to their immediate circumstances or else because they bear the scars of past traumas. Others may experience the less acute but persistent discomfort of ennui, a feeling of being limited or disillusioned by the way their lives have turned out. Still others feel fragmentation, like different parts of themselves are always at odds with one another. For me, it was alienation, like I was living from behind a glass bank-teller window that prevented me from fully experiencing my life. I longed for more connection, more presence.

Spirituality proposes to help us realize our own deepest being and to show us how we can embody that realization authentically in our lives. With such lofty promises, it's easy to get swept up in the hype; it's easy to project our fantasies onto spiritual teachers or to imagine that the particular tradition we are interested in is the one and only true path.

But that is not the kind of spirituality that's on offer in this book. Here, I will never ask you to leave your own judgment behind, to take anything on blind faith, or to sacrifice your own values or sovereignty. I will never ask you to dim your own light. Instead, we will approach the whole gamut of Asian spirituality with level-headed objectivity and common sense, and we will always prioritize your own individual values, goals, and experiences.

Does that sound like a useful approach? Is that the kind of spiritual exploration you'd like to embark on? If so, then grab your lamp and come along!

CHAPTER 1

PREPARING FOR THE JOURNEY

Have you ever seen those cartoons where the Western spiritual seeker has to climb to the peak of some faraway mountain in order to find a sagely master living in a cave to ask him the meaning of life? Well, that's not at all how it works anymore.

I'm using the metaphor of a spiritual journey throughout this book, but let's face it, no one in the modern world needs to engage in an arduous trek to the Himalayas or some other remote region of the globe in order to learn about Asian spiritual traditions. A simple Google search pulls up an Everest-sized mountain of reading material that you can peruse without ever leaving your living room couch. The whole spectrum is readily available, from Advaita and Buddhism to Yoga and Zen—and everything in between. Actually, these days, you don't even need to search for it to be bombarded with information on spirituality. It seems that at every turn it's there in books, magazines, podcasts, workshops, and even conversations among friends or coworkers. The problem with learning about Asian spiritual traditions today isn't that information is hard to find; it's information overload.

How Western people react to this information glut varies. (Note that in this book, when I say "Western people" I mean to refer to people of all races and backgrounds who have been raised primarily within the context of Western culture.) While Westerners with Asian family backgrounds are likely to have absorbed a variety of cultural influences, most of us have not had any deep exposure to

Asian traditions. Even fewer of us really get serious about exploring Asian spirituality, at best superficially engaging with memes and platitudes on social media or maybe buying a Buddha statue for the mantle. On the other hand, there are the "die-hards" who become long-term adherents of a particular sect or devotees of a particular guru. They commit themselves wholeheartedly to a particular Asian tradition and sometimes even pressure you to join them.

But what if you find yourself somewhere in the middle? You feel ready to travel beyond the superficial level but are not necessarily sure what the territory looks like. You're interested but also a bit skeptical. You are not feeling ready to commit to living in an ashram or monastery but feel a little curious about why someone might want to. You definitely want to investigate Asian spiritual traditions more deeply in order to get a clearer picture for yourself of what this world has to offer.

What do you do if you are a curious yet uncommitted spiritual explorer? Where do you turn for reliable information in English? Where can you get a map of the territory that is well-informed but accessible, serious but not overly dogmatic? With yoga studios on every street corner, hundreds of mindfulness apps to choose from, and Dalai Lama memes and Buddha quotes both real and fake constantly streaming into your social media feeds, where do you even start making sense of it all? In this dense forest of information, how can you learn to navigate toward what's authentic and avoid the baloney?

If that's the predicament you find yourself in, then I have good news. You are holding in your hands a guidebook that was written for explorers just like you. This book is going to cut through the noise and lay it all out for you. This is not just one more voice in an already crowded spiritual marketplace; here you've got a comprehensive map of the whole territory and a trusty guide who will show you how to navigate it.

This is a book for Western people who grew up without being steeped in Asian spiritual traditions and who do not have much previous experience in them. We are focused here on certain threads of spirituality that originated in the eastern half of Asia (from India to Japan) and that are today readily available in the West (so, no actual travel required). In a nutshell, we are focusing on various ideas and practices that have been drawn from Hinduism, Buddhism, Taoism, and other Chinese traditions that today are practiced globally. Some of the key ideas we'll cover in later chapters include mindfulness, yoga, Zen, nonduality, Tantra, chakras, vipassana, compassion practice, Taoism, martial arts, and Chinese medicine, among others.

How will we approach this material? Let me give you a basic road map. Here, in this first chapter, I provide you with essential orientation for the spiritual journey—answers to questions like, Where are we going? and Are spiritual claims for real? Chapter 2 then gives you some crucial background information for understanding Asian spirituality by laying out the history and doctrines of the major traditions. Chapters 3–6 are the core of the book, where I present a series of practices, detailing how to get started and what kinds of effects you can expect from long-term practice. (You can flip through those chapters if you want a quick sense of what kinds of things you'll take away from this book.) Chapter 7 ties together the previous four chapters by giving you my opinions on how to integrate these practices for optimal spiritual growth. Finally, chapter 8 digs into some thorny issues you may encounter as you further study Asian spirituality, such as cultural appropriation, bad translations, and more.

A BIT ABOUT YOUR GUIDE

Who am I to write a book like this? Why should you trust what I have to say? Those are good questions. We encourage a healthy dose skepticism around here!

Well, I'll start by telling you that I was not raised in an Asian culture or family context. I come from a transnational family that spans South America, Europe, and the US. My heritage is approximately 75 percent Latino, 90 percent European, 10 percent Indigenous

Amerindian, and precisely o percent Asian. I have studied Asian religions and cultures for most of my life through texts, travel, and deep immersion into practice, but I did not have the experience of growing up within that cultural milieu.

Further, although I have had a wide range of spiritual experiences, I make absolutely no claims to be enlightened or a sage within any particular spiritual tradition. Personally, I have always been allergic to gurus, and I have no interest in becoming one myself. But there's one kind of expertise I do have, which I will share with you here, and that's understanding the big picture of how all the Asian spiritual traditions fit together. In fact, you could say that that topic is my own personal specialty.

My interest in Asian spiritual traditions started when I was a kid. When I was in second grade, in 1981, I moved with my mother and siblings from Asunción, Paraguay, to a tiny rural community in New England (USA). There, I was mercilessly bullied by my peers for many years. To them, I was an outsider: different from everyone else and not welcome.

This was traumatic for me at the time, but I distinctly remember two things that gave me strength and solace in those days, both of which were connected with Asian spiritual traditions. The first was the idea of "the Force" from *Star Wars*. Don't laugh! It was the early 1980s, and the original trilogy of films—which were released in 1977, 1980, and 1983—was enormously popular with kids my age.

My young imagination was captivated by the idea that there was an invisible force that permeated the universe unifying all living beings. I knew the movie was fictional, but I couldn't help believing that you could train yourself to feel this energy and to use it to manipulate physical objects. I did not know until much later that the original *Star Wars* films were George Lucas's homage to old Japanese samurai films and that the idea of the Force was based on the East Asian concept of *qi* (also known as *ch'i* and *ki*—we'll say a lot more about this in chapter 6). But I remember lying awake in my bed for hours trying to find the Force by "stretching out with my feelings," just as Obi-Wan Kenobi instructed Luke Skywalker. And I do remember, once in a while, thinking that I felt something.

The second thing that really consolidated my interest in Asian spiritual traditions was the 1984 film *Karate Kid*. I totally related to the character of Daniel LaRusso, who was also the new kid in town and was also beaten up for being different. I longed for the kind of mentor that Daniel found in Mr. Miyagi and was fascinated by the martial arts techniques that he was learning. Of course, there's also the clincher at the end of the film, where Mr. Miyagi uses a mysterious energy that seemed to me a lot like the Force in order to heal Daniel and get him back into the competition ring. In the end, scrawny Daniel beats the bullies, wins the pretty girl's heart, and lives happily ever after. I was hooked!

Looking back, these films were problematic in some of the ways they played on stereotypes about Asia and Asians. I know now that they romanticized and exoticized aspects of Asian spirituality too. But at the time, these ideas had a powerful mystique, holding out an inspirational alternative to the painful status quo of my everyday life. They taught me that it might be possible to tap into invisible deeper layers of reality in order to find healing, power, and connection with the cosmos.

With those early seeds planted, by the time I was in high school I was training in two different forms of martial arts (one Korean and one Japanese) and dabbling in learning Chinese language too. I was reading voraciously about Asian religions—introductory books like *The Tao of Pooh*, dense primary texts like the *Upanishads*, and everything in between. Beginning in high school and into college, I also became intensely curious about Indigenous North and South American as well as European pagan spiritual traditions. I read the whole Carlos Castaneda series, Michael Harner's books on shamanism, the Gnostic Gospels, the works of Starhawk and Aldous Huxley, and much more. I experimented with astrology, ritual magic, and, ever so briefly, psychedelics. Nevertheless, all along, it was the Asian traditions that continued to speak to me most strongly, and in college I minored in East Asian studies to explore Buddhism and Taoism more methodically.

These interests came to a head after graduating from college, when I traveled with a friend to the Philippines and Indonesia. We were supposed to be two beach bums on a scuba diving vacation. However, from the moment we arrived in Southeast Asia, I felt that something deeper was calling me, like there was something important that I was supposed to be doing here. I had planned to return from the trip and to move to California to be a professional musician, but those plans quickly fell by the wayside. Instead, I found myself spending the next four years living in the city of Chiang Mai in northwestern Thailand. There, I became seriously engaged in learning about Buddhism and traditional Thai healing practices. I participated in numerous ten-day silent meditation retreats, spent several months in a Buddhist monastery, studied massage and herbal medicine at a traditional medicine hospital and in the living rooms of renowned master healers, and partic-ipated in many Buddhist and folk rituals within these different communities.

During those years, I took numerous side trips from Thailand, too, spending altogether about eight months in India, where I seriously studied yoga, Hindu-style meditation, and devotional chanting at an ashram in the Himalayan mountains; took a course in traditional Ayurvedic medicine in Southern India; and visited sacred sites all over the country. I also visited China, Malaysia, Singapore, and Mongolia. I learned aspects of Pranic Healing, Chinese medicine, spirit invocation, and a number of other techniques through a variety of workshops and teachers. I also had a few highly impactful mystical experiences during that time (one of which I describe in my previous book, *Buddhish*), which reinforced to me that there was something to this whole spirituality thing.

In 2001, after having been immersed in the practice of Asian spiritual and healing traditions for several years, I decided to return to the US to enroll in graduate school to study that subject in a formal academic setting and to make it the centerpiece of my life. I went back to the University of Virginia, where I had earned my undergraduate degree, and enrolled in the East Asian studies master's degree program. I went to school part time, while I also began a thriving practice as a therapist and teacher of Thai massage and herbal medicine. During that time I wrote several books about traditional Thai healing that were geared toward practitioners, but my own trajectory was already leaning in a different direction. The more time I spent in school, the more I realized that I was a natural-born scholar. I felt that I had finally discovered the most fruitful avenue for engaging in these Asian spiritual traditions that I loved so much.

My shift from being a practitioner to being a scholar was complete by 2005, when I enrolled in a PhD program at Johns Hopkins University's medical school to study the history of the connections between Buddhism and Asian medicine. Since that time, I have not engaged with patients or clients as a healer. Nor have I involved myself in intensive meditation or long-term yoga retreats in formal settings. Instead, I have dedicated the majority of my energy to the academic study of Asian religion and medicine.

While studying for my PhD, I learned how to read Buddhist texts from medieval China in their original language. Since that time, I have published many scholarly articles and books on the subject of "Buddhist medicine" in China and beyond. I have also continued to travel to Asia to research and observe many different aspects of Asian spiritual and healing traditions. I spent a year as a visiting scholar at a monastic university in Taiwan. I went back to Thailand for two fieldwork trips and rekindled my connection with various traditional doctors and folk healers. I spent a summer interviewing Buddhist healers in Korea and another summer doing the same on the West Coast of the US. I spent time touring religious and medical sites in Cambodia, Japan, and Vietnam. For years now, I have been the editor in chief of the leading academic journal for the humanistic study of Asian medicine. And I have taught many college courses on Buddhism, comparative Asian religions, Asian medicine, Asian history, and related topics.

I have also continued to experience profound spiritual insights and altered states of consciousness through my own personal practice over the years. But while this book is informed by these first-hand experiences, I am not writing it as a spiritual teacher or even as a model practitioner of any specific tradition. There was a span of a few years while I was living in Thailand in my twenties when I would have said I was Buddhist. Aside from that brief period, however, I have not been interested in adopting a single fixed spiritual identity or limiting myself to a single philosophy or practice. Instead, I am writing this book as someone who has a deep background in a lot of diverse traditions and practices. Someone who has done a lot of serious investigation of this topic in an up-close and personal way—there is nothing I have written about here that I haven't experienced for myself—but who, nonetheless, ultimately comes before you as a scholar and a critic.

Because of this, I believe I am an open-minded and objective guide to the terrain of Asian spiritual traditions. I have a ton of experience exploring this territory from different angles. I've done a lot of the practices, and they have meant a lot to me in my life. But I've also trained in the languages, studied the histories, and learned to separate the myths from the facts. I like to say that I am a student, friend, and fan of Asian spiritual traditions but also a researcher, a skeptic, and a critic. While I know a lot about these traditions, I'm more interested in what we can learn by comparing them all than I am in what we can learn by being a fundamentalist follower of just one.

Why am I talking about myself to this extent? I'm going through this personal history in detail because it shapes my presentation of the material in this book. You'll see that I switch between a scholarly voice (chapters 2 and 8) and a more conversational tone (3–7), wearing both of my hats as an academic and an experienced practitioner of Asian practices. However, throughout, I am always blending both perspectives because that's who I am and how I understand this material.

Also, my background informs my goals. Although this is not an academic book, my agenda here is an educational one. My purpose in writing this book is to educate Western people from all backgrounds and orientations about the broader world of Asian spiritual traditions, but to do so without requiring the reader to slog through scholarly prose or being pressured to accept any particular teachings as true. If this book can help to turn your curiosity about mindfulness, nonduality, the Tao, or Tantra—or some other thing you've heard about—into a greater awareness about how that concept fits into the richness and diversity of Asian spiritual traditions as a whole, then my mission has been accomplished.

WHAT ARE WE EXPLORING?

Before we get too far into this book, we've got to deal with a basic matter of definition. What does the word *spirituality* even mean? At the time I am writing this chapter, the following definition appears at the top of the *Wikipedia* page on spirituality, which I believe offers us a good starting point:

"Modern usages tend to refer to a subjective experience of a sacred dimension and the 'deepest values and meanings by which people live,' often in a context separate from organized religious institutions. This may involve belief in a supernatural realm beyond the ordinarily observable world, personal growth, a quest for an ultimate or sacred meaning, religious experience, or an encounter with one's own 'inner dimension.'"

In the US, where I live, people most often describe themselves as spiritual when they want to indicate that they have adopted certain ideas or practices related to the sacred, supernatural, and inner dimension of the self, while not being totally faithful to the dogmas of any particular religious tradition. Such people will sometimes use the whole phrase "spiritual not religious" to make this stance even clearer. Although individuals who identify in this way might attend a Buddhist meditation group or teach a particular brand of yoga in a local studio, for example, they typically avoid formally joining traditional religious congregations of Buddhists or Hindus. On the other hand, people who have officially converted to Buddhism and have formally joined a temple usually don't have a problem defining themselves as "Buddhist." Thus, using the word *spiritual* tends to suggest a certain looseness, flexibility, or eclecticism in someone's approach.

Western spiritual exploration of this kind has a long history, which we'll get into in more detail in chapter 2. Generally speaking, spiritual explorers have always been interested in healing, transcending, opening, deepening, integrating, and otherwise transforming themselves. And they value having the freedom to engage in a wide range of activities in pursuit of these goals. They are willing to experiment and to combine practices and ideas from different sources, while preferring not to lock themselves into any particular set of beliefs. Rather than adhere to religious dogma, they tend to use their own preferences and intuitions to mix these ingredients together in order to make their own distinctive blends of self-transforming practices. As we will see, the principal teachings of Asian spiritual traditions fit well with these goals and thus have been integral parts of spiritual exploration in the West for generations.

Buddhism, Hinduism, Taoism, and other Asian traditions all share the notion that human beings can engage in certain practices and adopt certain lifestyles that lead to a deeper and deeper understanding of themselves and the cosmos. All of these traditions explicitly refer to themselves as a "path" and promise that the end of the path will reveal the true, sacred, or divine nature of reality. Depending on the tradition, these paths are mapped out in ways that are simple or complex, straightforward or variable, secret or publicly known. But, ultimately, all Asian spiritual systems promise that there is some kind of perfected state, a point where we finally gain clear insight into the ultimate Truth, with a capital T. This state is held to be the pinnacle of what is possible for humans.

In English, we usually capture this ideal using the word *enlightenment*, but it's important to keep in mind that we are using this single word to translate many different Asian terms. In various traditions, an enlightened person is referred to as an *arhat*, a *buddha*, a *jivanmukta*, a *shengren*, a *xianren*, and so forth. In all cases, these terms indicate a person who has attained the highest level of realization. They are said to be perfectly wise, to do no harm, and to have become completely free from suffering. However, there are additional shades of meaning that diverge depending on the tradition. We will explore these differences in more detail in chapter 7.

Despite those divergences, our use of the single English word *enlightenment* often leads us to confuse Asian spiritual models with one another. In fact, in my experience, it is quite common among Western spiritual seekers who have relatively superficial exposure to Asian spiritual traditions to mix them up entirely. Based on an incomplete understanding, they often say things like "Buddhism, Hinduism, and Taoism are all essentially saying the same thing; they're like different roads leading up the same mountain." However, in my opinion as both a scholar and a practitioner, the differences are actually more striking—and more interesting—than the similarities. Once you spend a little time learning about all the diverse forms of Hinduism, Buddhism, Taoism, and other Asian spiritual traditions, you'll see that they share some basic ideas. But you'll also come to appreciate the differences more and more clearly.

Let me draw an analogy to food. People who are relatively unfamiliar with Chinese, Japanese, Korean, Thai, and Vietnamese cuisine might refer to all of it indiscriminately as "Asian food." Now, it is definitely true that there are some superficial similarities among these cuisines. It's true, for example, that all of them use soy sauce. But that certainly is not the most important detail about them, nor does it mean that they all taste the same! To someone with a bit more experience, there are important and obvious distinctions between these cuisines. The Japanese use of miso, the pungent blend of spices in Thai curries, and the Korean delicacy of kimchi have completely different flavor profiles and contribute to the diversity and uniqueness of each of their respective cuisines.

Once you have become familiar with the differences between them, you might feel that people who talk about Asian food as if it was all the same are not only factually wrong but perhaps also a bit offensive. Like, they can't be bothered to learn the differences. Well, it's the same thing with Asian spiritual traditions. When people assert that they're all just "different roads leading up to the same mountain," they are painting a drastically oversimplified picture. They're not doing justice to the individuality and unique contributions of each tradition, and in my opinion, they're being intellectually lazy.

We'll talk more about this issue in chapter 8. For now, please don't worry if you don't yet know enough to appreciate the different flavors of Asian spiritual traditions. That's precisely what this book is for. Here, we'll definitely talk about the similarities among traditions, but we will also spend a lot of time exploring the differences. In these pages, I'll introduce you to miso, curry, kimchi, and a dozen other flavors that are each unique and delicious in their own way. Maybe you'll become a connoisseur of Asian spiritual traditions, with an increasingly sophisticated palate and a hunger to taste more. Or maybe you'll realize that you just like one particular cuisine best of all and will decide to stick with that. What you ultimately do with the information presented here is up to you. But one thing is for sure: as we move forward, it will become clearer and clearer that Asian spiritual traditions are not all the same.

IS THIS JOURNEY FOR REAL?

Can people really become enlightened? Are spiritual ideas such as reincarnation, or that we all have a Buddha nature, or that we are all one with the universe, actually true? Is anything we'll be talking about in this book for real? Well, I should warn you right from the get-go that this book will not give you a definitive answer to those kinds of questions.

In order to explain my approach, let me introduce the distinction between *ontological truth claims* versus *phenomenological descriptions*.

Don't panic! These are just fancy academic terms for making claims about the way things *are* versus describing the way things *seem*.

Ontology is the branch of philosophy that is concerned with the question of what is fundamentally real. In my experience, most spiritual teachers and their students tend to make strong ontological claims about their own traditions. They preach to us that our current way of seeing the world is "an illusion" that needs to be abandoned, replaced, or upgraded. They promise that their particular philosophy describes "reality as it really is" or that their particular form of meditation or inquiry will show us our "true nature."

This book will describe the truth claims made by different traditions of Asian spiritual traditions, but you will notice that I will avoid making any such claims of my own. Throughout this book, I will be keeping an open mind about all ontological questions, and I will keep inviting you to do the same. While I will avoid making truth claims, however, I will not hesitate to offer you phenomenological descriptions of various spiritual states or insights. That means I will describe what sorts of experiences Asian spiritual teachings or traditions open up; what kinds of perceptions they help us discover; what new ways of seeing, hearing, and feeling they unlock for us. But I won't extrapolate from describing these experiences to making statements about ultimate reality.

No matter what your view of ultimate reality is, there's absolutely no doubt that Asian forms of spiritual practice can lead to some dramatic phenomenological shifts. For example, when I speak about the neo-Advaita style of self-inquiry in chapter 4, I will discuss how this form of practice can lead to a strange and transformative new way of perceiving oneself. Everything we previously knew about our place in the universe seems to flip inside-out. It suddenly seems blatantly obvious that there is no such thing as physical matter and that the only thing that's real in the universe is our own consciousness. However, in that part of the book, I will be underscoring that that is how it *seems*. I will not leap to making claims that this is how things actually *are*—although every neo-Advaita teacher I have ever heard does turn their phenomeno-logical experience into precisely that kind of truth claim.

Buddhists and Taoists also have their own teachings on ultimate reality, but we don't need to follow any one tradition's doctrinal train all the way to its ontological destination. Instead, we can discuss the phenomenology of these experiences—what it *seems like* to the practitioner who is having such experiences—without making any corresponding truth claims about how reality actually works.

I'm making a big deal of pointing out this distinction because it is probably the single most significant difference between this book and other resources on Asian spiritual traditions for practitioners. Virtually every book, website, podcast, or other piece of media written by a spiritual teacher from any tradition typically argues for the validity of their particular tradition's truth claims. Similarly, when spiritual explorers have profound individual experiences, they may extrapolate from those experiences to making truth claims about ultimate reality. For example, people who have had a near-death experience may argue that that *proves* the existence of life after death or God or some other mystical reality. Or people who have experienced memory of their past lives may argue that the fact they had this experience *proves* the existence of reincarnation.

Truth claims have the effect of pitting spiritual traditions against one another and against other systems of knowledge. Not only do Asian forms of spirituality differ from one another about the nature of reality, they also all diverge from the standard scientific worldview that most readers will have grown up learning in school. And, obviously, they are not the same as the monotheistic worldview of Judaism and Christianity that is so prevalent in Western culture either. If we approach our spiritual journey as an ontological inquiry, we are eventually going to be required to choose a single system as the one true description of what reality is really like and to reject the others. Or else, we will have to invent our own multiverse where all of these worldviews can be ultimately true simultaneously.

In this book, I take a different approach, side-stepping the issue of ultimate truth altogether. Why? Well, for starters, I personally don't believe that any religion or spiritual system has a perfect, infallible grasp on truth. My own opinion is that human beings can't possibly know the full, unvarnished, ultimate truth about reality. I believe that we are inherently limited by our bodies, senses, and minds to only ever being able to comprehend or perceive things from a limited and partial perspective. I also think it's impossible for humans to transcend our subjectivity in order to arrive at a totally clear picture of what is ultimately real. In other words, we are always stuck perceiving what it seems like, not what it is. Consequently, I prefer to always speak in an agnostic way on matters of ultimate truth, and I refrain from forcing my readers to make those choices either. I will report on the truth claims that are made by the traditions I talk about, but I won't present those views as truths in and of themselves.

Ultimate truth aside, I know from personal experience and from the written reports of thousands upon thousands of other people throughout history that human beings can indeed undergo profound phenomenological shifts in how we experience reality and ourselves through the spiritual practices discussed here. As we'll talk about in the upcoming pages, different practices are designed to elicit different kinds of phenomenological effects. While there is never any guarantee of success, when we sincerely put these techniques into practice over time, we greatly heighten the probability that we will experience these new perspectives. When those shifts come, these new viewpoints usually seem more vivid or more real than whatever ones we used to occupy. In fact, you might say that the definition of a mystical or spiritual experience is one that seems to be revealing a deeper truth about the universe than what you previously had access to. Nevertheless, in my view, it's always safest to conclude that that's just how things *seem*, not how things actually *are*.

At the end of the day, for our purposes in this book, it actually does not matter what you think is ultimately going on. For example, you might believe in a materialist worldview—that the effects of spiritual practice on your perception have to do with the way it rewires the neurons in your brain, for example. Or you might believe that an almighty god created the world and that spirituality is revealing a path that we can follow toward realizing his omni-presence. Or you might agree with the Buddhist assertion that spiritual realization has to do with how the practice of meditation clears out karmic accumulations that cloud your ability to clearly perceive your natural state. Or you might believe something else altogether. Because I focus on the phenomenology, you can believe whatever you want and still get a lot out of this book.

That being said, my opinion is that you'll get the most out of the discussion in these pages if you keep an open mind on matters of ultimate truth. I suggest taking your time investigating different spir-itual traditions, without feeling any pressure to jump to ontological conclusions. Even if you feel drawn toward one belief system over another, I encourage you to maintain an agnostic and even skeptical attitude rather than adopting a rigid conviction about what's real and what's not. That attitude, to me, is the very essence of an explorer's mindset and what differentiates us from die-hard religious devotees.

SETTING OUR COMPASSES

Before you embark, it's important to consider what direction do you want to walk on your spiritual journey. Different Asian models pro-vide different goals, expectations, and experiences for practitioners. So, before you commit to any particular practice, it's important to take a moment to ask where this particular path is headed. Do you know that its goals are a good fit for you? Are you aware of the range of experiences practitioners tend to undergo? Do you know where people wind up after years of long-term practice of it? In other words, my advice is not to just listen to promises a teacher or tradition is making about enlightenment, happiness, and bliss. Rather, closely examine the advanced practitioners of this system, and ask yourself if these are the outcomes you are looking for. Do they fit with what you want out of your life? Do they fit with your values?

If spiritual practice is a process of retraining yourself and re-tooling your life over the long term, think about what you are optimizing for. For example, if your spiritual practice is constantly giving you messages about how you need to "escape the entangle-ments" of money and social status, then that's how this practice will be shaping you day-to-day. On the other hand, if your practice is giving you messages about "manifesting" your spirituality through success and prosperity in worldly matters, then you'll be setting out on an entirely divergent course. The question is not which one of these two options is right but which one is right for you. For example, if you have a family and a career and care about being active in society, then getting involved in a form of spirituality that is strongly focused on "escaping entanglements" will cause tension with the rest of your life. Odds are the mismatch between your spirituality and your life will make you feel conflicted and tense instead of fulfilled and peaceful.

I learned this kind of lesson early on in my own spiritual ex-plorations. When I first encountered Theravada Buddhism while living in Thailand in my early twenties, I became quite enthralled with the practice of vipassana meditation (properly pronounced wee-PAH-sah-nah). I became fixated on my teacher's promise that serious, sustained practice of this kind of meditation would result in enlightenment. I wanted that for myself and applied myself diligently to the practice. For about four years, I was a veritable meditation junkie. I attended about a dozen ten-day retreats in Thailand, India, and elsewhere, and consistently meditated for two hours a day when not on retreat.

As we'll get into later in more detail, the particular form of meditation I was doing involves paying focused attention to the impermanent, dissatisfactory, and non-self nature of all human ex-periences. Predictably, over the time I was seriously doing this prac-tice, I gradually started to become more aloof and more detached from the world. I started feeling like the comings and goings of ordinary life were distractions from my practice. I felt that I could only truly be happy if I became a monk and lived in a monastery hidden away from the busyness of the world. But, yet, at the same time, I had grown up in a Latino family that placed a great deal of importance on staying connected. I also felt very attached to my girlfriend of many years, who I was living with in Thailand. The tug-of-war between my spiritual goals and my relationships caused a lot of stress for me (not to mention for my loved ones).

In the end, the desire for renunciation won out, and I chose to go live in a forest monastery in rural eastern Thailand. But as I get into in more detail in my previous book, *Buddhish*, not long after my arrival at the monastery I switched to practicing a different kind of meditation called *metta bhavana* (discussed in chapter 5). Instead of focusing on impermanence, non-self, and dissatisfaction, this practice involved mentally repeating positive affirmations of love and compassion for myself and all other beings. There was a lot of time for meditation at the monastery, and I practiced metta bhavana for many hours a day.

Wouldn't you know, in just a few weeks of immersing myself in metta, I had a heart-opening experience that was more mystical, powerful, and transformative than anything I ever experienced in years of diligent daily vipassana. The tension from the tug-of-war I'd been having with myself completely evaporated. I realized that I had been barking up the wrong tree for the past five years. I saw that vipassana was never actually a good fit for me, and that metta was much better aligned with my life and my values. Not only that, but this form of meditation came much more naturally to me than vipassana ever had. Vipassana had always felt like a chore to practice, but I felt joyful about practicing metta, even though I was doing so many more hours per day.

Fueled by this breakthrough, I left the monastery. I reconnected with my girlfriend, married her, started a family, enrolled in graduate school, and set out on the life trajectory that I am still on today. My interest in Buddhism switched from a passion for serious practice of Theravada (a style of Buddhism that is meditation focused) to a passion for scholarly research and teaching about Mahayana (a school of Buddhism that prioritizes compassion). I have never again thought about being a monk or going on an intensive vipassana retreat but instead threw myself into embodying compassion as a father, teacher, and member of my community.

To this day, I remember clearly when I went to the senior monk of the monastery to tell him that I had decided to leave after being there for just a few months. He looked at me gravely and told me how disappointing it was to hear that I was "giving up." He was convinced that I was making a huge mistake by succumbing to the "temptations" of the world outside.

I know plenty of meditators who would agree with him, and perhaps you are thinking the same thing too. But my firm position— which I'll reiterate countless times throughout this book—is that there is no one-size-fits-all system of spirituality. My realization in the forest was that the spirituality I had been practicing up to that point might be the best thing in the world for someone else, but it just wasn't right for me. I had struggled for years because I had oriented my compass in a direction that didn't work for me. As soon as I reset that trajectory in a direction that better jibed with my own life and values, the conflict quickly dissolved and things just clicked into place.

The point of my story is that as a spiritual explorer, you should take great care that when you set out on your journey, you actually want to walk in that direction. Don't lock yourself into one particular practice thinking it's the be-all and end-all; if the practice isn't resonating or the results aren't to your liking, then pull out your compass and set your bearing for another direction. Luckily for you, you're holding in your hands a comprehensive map that will give you the information you need to always ensure that you're informed about what lies ahead.

———

Great news! Our preliminaries have been taken care of, and we have been cleared to set out on our journey of exploration. The first stage of this expedition will be to visit all of the major traditions in order to hear a bit about the history, philosophies, and practices of each. Make sure you've got your suitcase packed, as we're about to quickly tour India, Southeast Asia, China, Tibet, and Japan.

Are you ready for the first leg of our adventure? Okay, then let's get going!

CHAPTER 2

SURVEYING THE TERRAIN

Every experienced trekker knows that before you set out on a serious hike you first need to survey the terrain. It's helpful to get the lay of the land by looking at some good maps—and it's even better if you have a knowledgeable tour guide alongside to point out the features and highlights of the territory. Luckily for you, you have both of those things.

My intention here is to briefly introduce you to the outlines of Hinduism, Buddhism, and East Asian spiritual traditions. We won't stop to take in all the details. Rather, it's as if we'll be flying over in an airplane to get a general sense of the whole landscape. Consider this chapter a rundown of the essential background information, concepts, and vocabulary you need to become a spiritual explorer of Asian traditions.

This is one of those chapters where I will don my scholarly hat. If you are dying to start practicing right away, I guess you could skip ahead to chapter 3. However, the current chapter provides essential background information for ideas and terminology you'll find throughout the rest of the book, so you may want to at least skim this chapter before jumping in.

For those of you who'd like to geek out further on the topics introduced here, at the end of this chapter I give you a list of suggested readings that can help you to dive into more details about history or read translations of historical sources. Another

jumping-off point for further research is to use the keywords introduced throughout this chapter to search through online resources
like Britannica.com. Just be aware that not all the information you
find on websites will be reliable! One of my hopes for this book
is that it can give you some basic outlines that will help you to
recognize when you are being led astray by misinformation. (I'll
say more about some of the most common misunderstandings in
chapter 8.)

WESTERN ENGAGEMENT WITH ASIAN TRADITIONS

As we begin our survey of the territory, the first thing we might
notice is that we are by no means the first Western people to have
walked this way. Western curiosity about Asian spirituality has a
very long history. Scholars of the ancient world tell us that substan-
tial cultural, artistic, scientific, and religious exchanges were taking
place between Greece and India as far back as the BCE period.
The Greek historian Strabo, who lived from around 64 BCE to
some time after 21 CE, described the beliefs and philosophies of
Indian yogis in his writings. Meanwhile, in Gandhara, northwestern
India, some of the first statues of the Buddha ever made, modeled
after the god Apollo, were created in the first centuries CE by
Indo-Greek artisans.

Such exchanges between East and West continued in subsequent centuries, intensified by the linking up of the trade networks
we now call the Silk Roads. A compelling example of this process of
exchange is the legend of the life of the Buddha. This story, which
originated in India, was adopted and retold as it spread westward
by followers of the Manichaean religion, then by Muslims, Jews,
and eventually Christians. By the eleventh century, the story was
being retold in Europe as "The Tale of Barlaam and Josaphat."
The source of the story remained unknown, until eventually, both
Barlaam and Josaphat were made into Christian saints. Yes, you
read that right: the Buddha, under the name St. Josaphat, is to this
day one of the saints recognized by the Orthodox church!

Going the other way, there were Christian churches in China as early as the seventh century CE and Jewish settlements in India by the ninth. Because the continents have been so interlinked for so long, there are many similarities between medieval European and Asian religious and spiritual traditions. All over the region, people prayed to divine beings who were depicted with halos of light above their heads, counted their prayers on strings of beads, used holy water to give blessings, told similar myths, and exhibited countless other commonalities in practice and doctrine.

Although they were numerous, premodern examples of cross-cultural exchange from Asia to Europe tended to happen under the radar, so to speak. Christianity was always vehemently opposed to Asian religions, labeling them as "heathen," "idolatrous," and "barbaric." When eventually they were in a position to do so, Western Christians often took steps to eradicate or disempower adherents. Early in the period of British colonial occupation of India (1757–1947), for example, colonial authorities labeled yoga as a subversive and backward practice, and Indian yogis were persecuted and jailed. (Check out Mark Singleton's book *The Yoga Body* for the fascinating details.)

Attitudes were no different in the US. Significant numbers of Asian people began arriving in the Western part of the US in the middle of the nineteenth century as a result of the gold rush and the building of the transcontinental railroad, and they also moved to Hawaii in the same era to work on sugar plantations. Members of these Asian American communities practiced the religious traditions of their home countries under the disdainful eye of their Christian neighbors. Buddhism, Taoism, and other Asian expressions of spirituality were looked down upon as un-American and backward. (The film *Aloha Buddha* is a great source for these details.)

Although prejudice against the practice of Asian spiritual traditions persisted in these ways, some white people did enthusiastically embrace and even promote them. Beginning in the late nineteenth century, Transcendentalists such as Ralph Waldo Emerson (1803–1882) and Henry David Thoreau (1817–1862) were among the first popular Western authors to be captivated by Asian spirituality. The Theosophical Society, founded in 1875 by the Russian mystic known as Madame Blavatsky (1831–1891), was an influential international organization dedicated to incorporating Asian ideas and practices into Western spiritual practice. It was particularly instrumental in promoting the Hindu saint Ramakrishna (1836–1886). Other important proponents of Hindu traditions in North America in the early twentieth century included Sri Aurobindo (1872–1950), Paramahansa Yogananda (1893–1952), and Jiddu Krishnamurti (1895–1986).

Once those floodgates opened, successive waves of Asian spiritual traditions entered the Western mainstream in succeeding decades. In the 1950s, Westerners were introduced to Zen Buddhism through the Beat writers such as Jack Kerouac (1922–1969) and Allen Ginsberg (1926–1997), as well as through the popular writings of the Japanese authors D. T. Suzuki (1870–1966) and Shunryu Suzuki (1904–1971). In the late 1960s, the Beatles began promoting the Indian guru and founder of Transcendental Meditation, Maharishi Mahesh Yogi (1918–2008), and began working Hindu lyrics into some of their popular songs. The 1970s and '80s saw the rising popularity of charismatic white gurus such as Ram Dass (1931–2019) as well as Indian gurus such as Bhagwan Shree Rajneesh aka Osho (1931–1990), who injected the New Age movement with aspects of Hindu spirituality. Meanwhile, high-profile teachers such as Chögyam Trungpa (1940–1987) and the Fourteenth Dalai Lama (1935–) sparked an interest in Tibetan Buddhist practices in increasingly wider segments of the population. Mindfulness and vipassana—forms of meditation largely derived from Southeast Asian Buddhism—began to be increasingly connected with well-being and positive lifestyle changes by teachers like S. N. Goenka (1924–2013), Thich Nhat Hanh (1926–2022), and Jack Kornfield (1945–).

By the end of the twentieth century, many aspects of Asian spirituality had become well known across the English-speaking world. Sanskrit words such as *karma*, *nirvana*, and *yoga* had become household terms. Forms of meditation such as TM, Zen, vipassana, and mindfulness had become mainstream practices. Chinese medicine had become legally recognized, and the Tao had become a major cultural touchstone. All of these practices and ideas were circulating widely on the internet, allowing an increasing number of people of non-Asian backgrounds to be able to experiment with the whole range of Asian spiritual traditions.

By this time, Asian practices had also caught the attention of psychologists and medical researchers. While some of this research began in the early twentieth century, the first decades of the twenty-first century saw an explosion of serious psychological and medical studies. Research findings linking mindfulness, yoga, tai chi, qigong, reiki, and other practices with improved mental and physical health have been widely reported in the popular media. This has led to even more popularity for Asian spiritual traditions among the general public. (At the time of this writing, in October 2024, for example, the comprehensive medical research database PubMed includes over 8,500 research articles with "mindfulness" in the title, 4,400 with "yoga," and 1,600 with "tai chi.")

That is not to say that any of this enthusiasm for Asian *spirituality* has led to the widespread adoption of the *religions* of Hinduism, Buddhism, or Taoism in the West. Of course, Westerners with Asian heritage often grow up going to temples or participating in regular religious practices at home with their families and may continue to identify as belonging to these religions as adults. But it is fairly rare for Westerners who are not Asian to formally convert to these religions. Thus, the percentage of Westerners who identify as adherents of Asian religions remains vanishingly small. According to the 2020 US census, while 6.2 percent of Americans identify as Asian, only 0.7 percent of the population identify as Buddhist or Hindu when asked their religion. The "Eurobarometer" study, conducted by the European Commission in 2021, revealed that 0.6 percent of EU residents identified as Buddhist and only 0.1 percent as Hindu. Taoists did not even register on either poll.

Nevertheless, although Westerners aren't necessarily flocking to join Asian religions in any formal way, they are enthusiastically adopting a range of techniques, practices, and ideas that derive from those religions. Today, a lot of these ideas and practices have become well-known thanks to the global spiritual marketplace. In the rest of this chapter, I will walk you through how these originated, how they developed over time, and how they were eventually extracted from their original cultural contexts, "unbundled" from religious doctrines, and spread globally for spiritual explorers everywhere to engage with in the twenty-first century.

HINDUISM

Hinduism is often called the world's oldest religion. Surprisingly, however, the term *Hinduism* only came into use as a name for a set of religious ideas and practices in the early nineteenth century. Once the term was accepted, Hinduism brought diverse practitioners all over India together into a shared religious identity that emphasized their commonalities. Prior to that time, however, these disparate groups of practitioners primarily identified as followers of specific sects or traditions—as Shaivas, Vaishnavas, Tantrikas, and so forth—and not really as part of a larger unified whole.

Today, even though we have this inclusive term, I think it is still better to understand Hinduism as a family of traditions rather than as a single religion. Of course, these traditions share some common reference points: the caste system was a major tool of social organization throughout Indian history; the ancient language of Sanskrit was used for sacred writing and speech in most times and places; the notion of *karma*, or the cycle of rebirth based on one's ethical merits, was near universally accepted; the term *dharma* was normally used to refer to the proper way of living and behaving regardless of who was promulgating that viewpoint and what lifestyle they were advocating. However, despite those similarities, there isn't a unified theoretical or philosophical basis that ties together all forms of Hinduism. Additionally, we should note that most of these major concepts also play just as big a role in Jainism and Buddhism, two traditions that also originated in ancient India but which were never folded into the broader category of Hinduism.

The earliest sacred texts associated with Hinduism are the *Vedas*, a collection of four principal scriptures plus commentaries and other related texts that were composed a very long time ago. The oldest of these texts, the *Rigveda*, has been dated to around 3,200–3,500 years ago, and it is certainly one of the oldest sacred texts still in use today.

While the *Vedas* are revered and chanted by many contemporary Hindus, other later texts are just as influential. The *Upanishads*, a set of teachings composed 600–300 BCE, are often referred to as "Vedanta" ("the culmination of the *Vedas*"). These short scriptures contain the earliest descriptions of yogic philosophy and practice. The *Ramayana*, created in the first millennium BCE, and the *Mahabharata*, from the third century BCE to the third century CE, are two great epics that have been major sources shaping Indian religions as well as dance, theater, and many other aspects of culture. A portion of the latter text, separately titled the *Bhagavad Gita*, is likely the most well-known Hindu religious scripture outside of India, and it has been translated and discussed in numerous publications in English, including by such prominent Hindus as Mahatma Gandhi (1869–1948). Finally, the *Puranas*, written primarily in the first millennium CE, is a rich collection of sources filled with myths and legends about the gods and goddesses.

Because of the diversity of traditions under the Hindu umbrella, it is difficult to decide how to present them succinctly in a short overview like this one. But one way that may work for our purposes is to group them into three general approaches to religious practice—devotion, yoga, and nonduality—since each of these has been widely embraced in the West.

Devotion to deities has been the most dominant form of practice throughout the history of Hinduism. This is first seen in the Rigveda and continues to be a mainstay of practice for most Hindus today. Hinduism is a polytheistic religion, meaning it recognizes a multiplicity of gods, goddesses, and other deities. Over time, a consolidation process took place whereby minor and local deities came gradually to be thought of as "manifestations" or "avatars" of major gods and goddesses. Some of the most prominent deities are Shiva, lord of the ascetic practices of the yogis; Vishnu, the protector of the cosmic order; Hanuman, the monkey god known for his strength and loyalty; Ganesha, the elephant-headed remover of obstacles; and Shakti, the divine feminine power. Because of the process of consolidation, many of these deities have numerous manifestations. Vishnu, for example, is an amalgamation of at least ten avatars, a list that includes the gods Rama and Krishna—each of whom are in and of themselves major deities. Shakti also has many manifestations, including Durga, the slayer of demons; Kali, goddess of death; Lakshmi (or Laxmi), patroness of wealth and success; and Saraswati, patroness of knowledge, language, and the arts.

Each of the Hindu deities has their own particular set of prayers, offerings, rituals, mantras (a Sanskrit word meaning a chant or incantation), and other actions that devotees perform, and they often have their own separate temples. Devotees tend to focus on certain deities over others. Often such choices have to do with one's village or family traditions, but they can also represent personal choice or a "calling" to work with a particular deity. Usually, Hindus include multiple deities in their devotional practice, appealing to different gods and goddesses on different occasions and for different reasons.

In modern times, many of the Hindu gods have been embraced in the West. Sometimes, their images are used for crass marketing purposes that are offensive and disrespectful. However, it is also true that many Western practitioners incorporate the more popular Hindu deities into their spirituality in more earnest and respectful ways. While Western people who did not grow up in Hindu families are less likely to participate in formal devotional worship, one major exception is the Hare Krishna movement. Focused on ceremonial devotion for the god Krishna, this movement held a major place in the Western spiritual scene in the 1960s and '70s.

Founded in 1966 in New York City, the International Society for Krishna Consciousness is now an international organization with a million members worldwide.

A second major approach to Hindu practice is yoga. Meaning "union" or "connection," most English speakers think that this Sanskrit word refers to physical exercises that stretch the body. However, in a Hindu context, the term is much more expansive, referring in general to a whole range of mental and physical practices. What these practices all have in common is that they are designed to bring one into union or connection with the divine. For yogis, it's not enough to be devoted to the divine, or to attend temple and pray. The goal is to experience the divine for—or better yet, within—oneself.

We'll have a lot more to say about different kinds of yoga in the coming chapters. For now, let's just make a few historical notes. The earliest scriptures with yogic content are the previously mentioned *Upanishads*, which describe breathing exercises, meditations, chanting the mantra OM, the subtle energies that animate the bodymind, and a number of other ideas. Over the centuries after the *Upanishads* were written, yogic approaches like these continued to be practiced. However, they were not always preserved in texts, perhaps because they were primarily considered to be secret oral transmissions from teacher to student.

After the *Upanishads*, the next major text to detail the practice of yoga was the *Yoga Sutras*, written by Patañjali around 400 CE. This text systematized the practice of yoga into eight disciplines or "limbs." These eight included moral restrictions, virtues one should cultivate, physical postures, breathing exercises, withdrawal of the senses, concentration, meditation, and absorption. Many of these terms are open for interpretation, and exactly what they mean has been debated for many centuries. However, it is clear that Patañjali's purpose was to present a comprehensive yogic system that aimed at enlightenment through the combination of ethics and mind-body cultivation. (It is also clear that his system was very much influenced by Buddhism, which had been teaching an eight-limb system of personal transformation using many of the same technical Sanskrit terms for about eight hundred years before Patañjali. More on that in the next section.)

Aside from the *Upanishads* and the *Yoga Sutras*, there are few other major texts from the ancient period that describe yoga practice in any detail. However, a movement called Tantra, which emerged around 600 CE, changed all of that. Tantra was an enormously popular development that eventually affected all Asian religions. The Tantric movement left us a voluminous amount of sources, which recorded and systematized yogic practices in much more detail than ever had been done before.

As with the *Upanishads* and the *Yoga Sutras*, the goal of Tantric practice was to cultivate the whole bodymind in pursuit of enlightenment. Tantric texts (called *tantras*) talk about how practitioners could use meditation, mantras, visualization, breath, and physical postures alongside other forms of ritual practices in order to affect the subtle energies. Some tantras talk about sexuality as an arena in which a practitioner could work on mental and physical cultivation. Others focus on what scholars call "antinomian practices"—practices such as smearing one's body with cremation ashes—that were intentionally designed to break cultural taboos.

Certain branches of Shaiva Tantra (forms of Tantra associated with the Hindu god Shiva) further elaborated the practices introduced in the *Upanishads* and the *Yoga Sutras*, developing what became known as *Hathayoga*. Meaning "forceful yoga," these practices became identified as a direct and effective way of manipulating the energy body in order to achieve enlightenment. The more influential texts from this movement were composed between the eleventh and seventeenth centuries. These texts present the combination of physical postures, breathing exercises, chakras, kundalini, and spiritual goals that are still the basis of some forms of modern yoga.

Truth be told, however, the vast majority of contemporary yoga practices has jettisoned the whole idea of enlightenment. The religious priorities of premodern yoga have been replaced with a secular perspective that thinks of yoga simply as a practice for stress reduction and health. The history of how this transformation took place goes back to the late 1800s, when the physical dimension of Hathayoga (the *asanas*, or postures) was adopted as a cross-training by Indian competitive bodybuilders. From there, yoga found its way into YMCAs and other gyms around the world. Twentieth-century yoga gurus such as Swami Sivananda (1887–1963), K. Pattabhi Jois (1915–2009), B. K. S. Iyengar (1918–2014), and others developed distinct styles or brands of yoga training that became immensely popular in the West, contributing to the commercialization of the practice.

While a lot of yoga in the West today is secularized and disconnected from any spiritual goals, there still are a few schools of yoga that introduce Westerners to a range of Tantric practices as part of their training system. These include forms of Hathayoga and Kashmiri Shaivism. In addition, there has been quite a bit of Western interest in practicing Tantric sexuality, sometimes called neo-Tantra, since the 1960s. Another globally popular Hindu practice, Transcendental Meditation, uses mantra meditation to cultivate spiritual insights as well as *siddhis*, magical powers such as levitation that are associated with spiritual awakening in many Hindu traditions.

Finally, we can discuss a third major approach to Hindu practice, which can loosely be labelled as *advaita* (pronounced add-WAI-tah, with emphasis on the second syllable), or "nonduality." Broadly speaking, advaita refers to a philosophical position that holds that the individual self (*atman*) is none other than the divine absolute reality (*brahman*). Elements of this kind of philosophy can also be identified in the Upanishads as well as in some of the medieval schools of yoga. Advaita Vedanta, a philosophical school that traces its founding to Adi Shankara around the eighth century CE, became the most influential form of this tradition. Advaita Vedanta was first popularized in the West by the internationally famous Hindu monk, or swami, Vivekananda (1863–1902).

In the nineteenth and twentieth centuries, advaita philosophy was the cornerstone of the teachings of Ramana Maharshi (1879–1950), and his successor, H. W. L. Poonja (aka Papaji, 1910–1997). These two teachers articulated a practice, now known as neo-Advaita, which focused on the practice of self-inquiry in order to achieve direct realization of the non-separation of self and the absolute. I'll have much more to say about this practice in chapter 4. The thing to emphasize at the present moment is that neo-Advaita focuses on facilitating a profound awakening experience through a direct shift in consciousness. Unlike yogic practice, which addresses the cultivation of the entire bodymind, neo-Advaita pays no attention to the body nor does it have much to say about devotional practice or deities. Many Westerners are attracted to this form of spirituality, which often claims to be a fast or "direct" method of realization, as opposed to the slower path of cultivation represented by yoga.

And that, my friends, brings us to the end of our brief tour of Hinduism. Please remember that dividing historical and modern Hinduism into these three currents of devotion, yoga, and non-duality is only one way of approaching this material. I also want to reiterate that we are merely scratching the surface and that it is impossible to comprehensively cover all of the various ideas and practices that make up the rich tapestry of Hinduism in a few pages. My goal is simply to cover the key terms and historical points in an efficient way for our present purposes. Please see the additional resources at the end of this chapter if you're left wanting to dive in deeper and learn more.

Throughout this chapter, I will also provide excerpts from some core texts from Hinduism, Buddhism, and Taoism that express succinctly some of the main religious or philosophical commitments of each tradition. I have given you the sources that these translations come from, so that you can enjoy looking through additional passages from these sacred Asian classics.

BOX 2.1: *Chandogya Upanishad,*
Chapter 6, Sections IX and XIII

Translated by Max Müller (at sacred-texts.com), with my edits.

The following two passages come from one of the earliest statements of nonduality within Hindu tradition. Here, a boy named Svetaketu is being tutored by his father, using a series of metaphors in order to explain the nonduality between the divine nature of the self (here capitalized as Self) and all of life.

IX.

"My son, bees make honey by collecting the juices of distant trees and reduce the juice into one form. And as these juices have no discrimination, they cannot say, 'I am the juice of this tree or that.' In the same manner, my son, all creatures, when they have become merged into the True, know not that they are merged in the True. Whatever these creatures are here, whether a lion, or a wolf, or a boar, or a worm, or a midge, or a gnat, or a mosquito, they become that again and again. But that which is the subtlest essence, all that exists has its self in that. It is the True. It is the Self. And you, Svetaketu, are that. . . . "

XIII.

"Place this salt in water, and then come to me in the morning."

The son did as he was commanded.

The father said to him: "Bring me the salt, which you placed in the water last night."

The son looked for it, but found it not, for of course it was dissolved.

The father said: "Taste it from the surface of the water. How is it?"

The son replied: "It is salty."

"Taste it from the middle. How is it?"

The son replied: "It is salty."

"Taste it from the bottom. How is it?"

The son replied: "It is salty." . . .

Then the father said: "Here also, in this body, you do not perceive the True, my son; but there indeed it is. That which is the subtlest essence, all that exists has its self in that. It is the True. It is the Self. And you, Svetaketu, are that. . . . "

BUDDHISM

Buddhism originated in northeastern India somewhere in the middle of the first millennium BCE. We do not know very much about the person who founded this tradition other than what is said in the traditional legends about his life. According to those myths, Siddhartha Gautama was the crown prince of a small kingdom who renounced his obligations, his wealth, his throne, and his family in order to become a spiritual explorer.

Once he left home, the story goes, Siddhartha studied with a number of famous teachers, specifically focusing on mastering yogic approaches. But he found that even the most exalted states of bliss and nondual union he achieved with these practices did not fully eradicate suffering. Because of this, Siddhartha eventually rejected all of these teachings and decided to set his own course. Sitting under a tree in the forest one night, he discovered a new method of meditation that led to a deeper, fuller enlightenment than what he had found through those other techniques. He called the end result of his meditation *nirvana* (literally meaning "cessation"; see chapter 4).

The Buddha's teachings preserved many ideas and orientations from Hinduism. He took for granted the reality of reincarnation and agreed with the common idea that the main goal of religious practice should be to escape the cycle of rebirth. However, there are some major differences between Buddhist teachings and Hinduism. Some of these differences have to do with challenging social norms. For example, Buddhism rejected the Indian caste system, allowing people of high or low origin to join the monastic order with equal rank. Buddhism also rejected the male-centered religiosity of Hinduism, allowing women to become ordained religious practitioners (although it should be noted that they were only ever allowed second-class citizenship in the order).

The Buddha's teachings were carried orally for several centuries as they spread around the Indian subcontinent, until they eventually began to be written down in the first century BCE. These texts, generically referred to as *sutras*, were written in the ancient Indian languages of Pali and Sanskrit. Unlike some genres of Indian religious literature, which can be quite sparse in detail, the sutras lay out Buddhism's teachings systematically. These doctrines are often enumerated: the Three Marks of Existence, the Four Noble Truths, the Eightfold Noble Path, the Twelve Links of Dependent Origination, and so forth. This does tend to make understanding Buddhist doctrine a bit overwhelming for the newcomer, but it also makes things easier to remember.

The main idea across all of these texts and doctrines is the refutation of the Hindu notion that the self is synonymous with a divine absolute reality. As we'll explore in detail in chapter 4, Buddhism's notion of truth is also nondual, but it approaches nonduality from the opposite direction by asserting that neither the separate self nor an eternal divine absolute exists. The practices required to achieve realization of this truth, which is called "non-self" (*anatta*) or "emptiness" (*sunyata*), involve renunciation of the worldly life and dedicating oneself to serious meditation. The sutras describe many forms of meditation, including mindfulness (*sati*) and insight meditation (*vipassana*), which are both geared toward understanding ultimate reality, as well as loving-kindness meditation (*metta bhavana*), which is designed to help one cultivate compassion for oneself and others. We will get into all of these practices in more detail in subsequent chapters.

Buddhism is a monastic religion, and most Buddhist thought leaders throughout history have been monks. These monks have historically placed a lot of attention on scholasticism, textual study, and philosophical rigor. Throughout the millennia since the Buddha's lifetime, Buddhist monks have distilled and built upon the stories, information, and meditations presented in the scriptures in order to develop more and more detailed models of practice. Some of the leading synthesizers of the Buddhist tradition as it developed in India were Ashvaghosa, Nagarjuna, Asanga, Vasubandhu, Buddhaghosa, Dharmakirti, Chandrakirti, and Shantideva, whose dates span the first millennium CE.

While Hinduism spread beyond India to a few places like Cambodia and Indonesia, it was far more successful in India than abroad.

The opposite applies for Buddhism. Buddhism was enormously popular in India for the first thousand years of its existence. Yet, by about 1200 CE, it had been almost completely displaced by Hinduism. However, as early as the first century CE, Buddhist writings, art, culture, and practices had all begun to be transmitted along the Silk Roads and other trade routes that connected India with Asia. Thus, by the time Buddhism had largely died out in India, it had been transplanted to many other places and the sutras had been translated into many other languages. Buddhism thrived across Southeast, East, and Central Asia and the Himalayas, and it continues to do so to the present day.

Everywhere that Buddhism traveled it was transformed through contact with local cultures and ways of life. Different schools of Buddhism came to predominate in different areas. Theravada ("the Teachings of the Elders") was most widespread in Southeast Asia. This type of Buddhism emphasizes the need to follow in the footsteps of the Buddha, to leave ordinary life behind and become a monk or nun, to practice meditation diligently, and to liberate oneself from suffering. However, it has always been the case that the vast majority of Theravada Buddhists have been laypeople who do not devote themselves to full-time meditation. In fact, most lay Buddhists do not meditate at all. For them, Theravada offers a whole range of rituals and practices that can provide protection, good luck, and other magical benefits. They often engage in practices to earn meritorious karma, so they can be reborn in better and better circumstances—and perhaps eventually become enlightened some day far in the future.

The second major division of Buddhism, Mahayana ("the Great Vehicle") is a family of different traditions that is so diverse and inclusive that it is hard to generalize about it. Some common features of Mahayana are a strong emphasis on compassion and generosity, as well as a wide range of devotional practices focused on deities. Rather than exclusively following his meditation instructions, Mahayana Buddhists also believe that Siddhartha Gautama is one of many Buddhas and bodhisattvas (powerful beings with godlike powers) who can be prayed to and asked for help in daily life. Some of the most popular Mahayana bodhisattvas that you might be familiar with are Budai (the so-called Fat Buddha) and Guanyin (also known as Kwan Yin or the Goddess of Mercy).

The majority of Mahayana Buddhists throughout history have lived in East Asia (China, Japan, Korea, Taiwan, and Vietnam), and one significant Mahayana tradition in that part of the world is Pure Land Buddhism. This school of practice involves praying to Amitabha (the Buddha of Infinite Light) for rebirth in his paradise realm—in a way not wholly dissimilar from how Christians hope to have an afterlife in Heaven.

Another popular form of Mahayana is Zen. This tradition has a strong focus on meditation, which is what the word *zen* actually means. In medieval Japan, Zen was associated with the samurai military class, so Japanese Zen often focuses on self-discipline and has a notably spartan aesthetic. It is also in Zen that we find Buddhism's deepest appreciation for nature and the simple joys of ordinary life. The recently deceased Buddhist peace activist and popularizer of mindfulness Thich Nhat Hanh was a proponent of Vietnamese Zen whose teachings frequently focused on these topics. His beautiful writings also tend to highlight Mahayana Buddhism's notions of interdependence (that everything in the universe is dependent upon and interconnected with everything else).

The third major division of Buddhism is most often called Vajrayana ("the Vajra vehicle"), named after a magical tool that symbolizes rapid transformation. Vajrayana grew out of Mahayana and considers itself the culmination of that tradition. However, because of its differences with mainstream Mahayana, it is usually considered to be a distinct school or branch on the Buddhist family tree. There are forms of Vajrayana in East Asia, Mongolia, Bhutan, and Nepal, but the most influential and best known in the West are the ones that developed in Tibet.

Tibetan Buddhism is in and of itself an extremely diverse family of sects and approaches. There are four main schools: Nyingma, Kagyu, Sakya, and Gelug. (The Fourteenth Dalai Lama, who is by far the best-known Buddhist living today, is often thought to be some kind of "Buddhist Pope," but he is really just the leader of the Gelug school.) There is considerable debate among these schools on various points of philosophy, as well as on how one should practice. In general, in Vajrayana there is often an idea that one should start by practicing the kinds of meditation advocated by Theravada Buddhism, move on to those advocated by Mahayana, and ultimately graduate to the advanced meditations that are taught only by the Vajrayana schools.

Upper-level Vajrayana practices are normally kept secret from the general population and are taught only to people who have taken certain vows and have undergone ritual initiations called "empowerments." Vajrayana is a Tantric form of Buddhism, which was influenced by the same pan-Indian movement that brought forth Tantric Hinduism. Therefore, the upper-level Vajrayana practices are similar to the practices of yoga: working with energy in order to produce a fully embodied enlightenment. (See chapter 6 for more details.)

All three of these major forms of Buddhism are widespread in the West today. Most of the kinds of mindfulness meditation that have become so popular derive from Theravada Buddhism. Meanwhile, Mahayana is by far the most significant tradition among Asian immigrants to the West. And, finally, while there are only a small number of Tibetans living in the West, Tibetan Buddhism has attracted a large number of non-Asian practitioners and the Dalai Lama is a genuine celebrity. Given all of their doctrinal and social differences, these groups have only minimal contact with one another. However, leaders and partisans of these different Buddhist sects rarely exhibit public conflicts or tensions.

And here concludes our quick tour of Buddhism. From this brief sketch, I think you can appreciate that Buddhism—like Hinduism—is not one thing but rather a diverse family of different approaches and ideas. Originating in the teachings of one Indian spiritual explorer, Buddhism spread all across Asia, intermixed with many other cultural influences, and developed in countless locally specific ways. I'm sure you can imagine that all of these various

BOX 2.2: *The Discourse on Evidence of Selflessness*
(Anatta-lakkhana Sutta)

Translated by Glenn Wallis in *Basic Teachings*
of the Buddha (Random House, 2007)

In this brief excerpt from the ancient Pali collection of sacred Buddhist texts, the Buddha teaches his monks about his fundamental principle of non-self. Here, the Buddha identifies five things that people may think of as a self and instructs the monks to see them "with right understanding" as not constituting a self after all.

Whatever body there is—whether past, present, or future; internal or external; subtle or massive; inconsequential or exalted; close at hand or in the distance—every body should be seen with thorough understanding for what it is: *This is not mine, I am not this, this is not my self.*

Similarly, whatever feeling, perception, conceptual fabrications, and cognizance there are—whether past, present, or future; internal or external; subtle or massive; inconsequential or exalted; close at hand or in the distance—each of these should be seen with a thorough understanding for what it is: *This is not mine, I am not this, this is not my self.*

Seeing in this way, as a trained practitioner, you become disenchanted with the body, feeling, perception, conceptual fabrications, and cognizance. Being disenchanted, you are free from infatuation. Because of this dispassion, you are liberated.

forms of Buddhism don't necessarily always jibe with one another, and it's true that there is often contradiction between Buddhist groups over even the most basic doctrines. If you're interested in learning more, consult my book *Buddhish* or the recommended books at the end of this chapter.

CHINESE TRADITIONS

In the previous section on Buddhism, I talked about the Mahayana forms of Buddhism that have been very popular in East Asia. But Buddhism came to the region from India. In this section, we are focusing on traditions that are native to China.

One of the oldest texts in Chinese history, and no doubt also the most influential overall, is the *I-Ching* (also spelled *Yijing*; see box 2.3 for a note on spelling discrepancies and tips on pronunciation). First written by an anonymous author around 1000–750 BCE, the *I-Ching* is a divination text used to understand the present and foretell the future.

To use this oracle, people draw yarrow stalks or, more often today, flip coins in order to draw out two trigrams made of solid or broken lines. These trigrams are combined into a hexagram, and the book lists all sixty-four possible hexagram combinations with short poems and commentaries illuminating their meanings. It is impossible to overstate how influential this method of divination has been throughout Chinese history. It continues to be consulted today by Chinese people the world over, both in the old-fashioned way and through smartphone apps and websites.

Another ancient source of Chinese spiritual wisdom, though not quite as old as the *I-Ching*, is the philosophy of Taoism (also spelled Daoism). This school of thought began in China around 400 BCE. This was around the time when many of the major schools of Chinese philosophy were founded. As China was not yet unified, philosophers competed for attention and patronage from the various royal courts. Taoism offered something different from its main competitor, Confucianism, which was championed by Confucius (551–479 BCE) and Mencius (371–289 BCE).

Whereas Confucianism and other schools talked about how the ruler should wield power and shape the populace, Taoism advocated a philosophy of "non-doing" or "non-action" (*wuwei*). Rather than advising practitioners to be skilled in warfare, politics, statecraft, and administration, Taoism taught that the sagely person should be frugal, simple, humble, laid back, and carefree. One should learn to go with the flow of life, referred to as the Tao (or the Dao, literally meaning "the Way"). Someone in harmony with the Tao lived life without resistance, like how a stream of water effortlessly flows around rocks.

BOX 2.3: Pronunciation of Chinese Terms

There is considerable confusion among non-Chinese speakers about the pronunciation of many of the Chinese terms in this section. This is due to the fact that there are different ways of transcribing the Chinese language—that is to say, different ways of spelling out Chinese words in the English alphabet. An older system that was used up to the late twentieth century was replaced with a system that fixed some of the problems but also introduced new ones. Throughout this book I will be using whichever spelling of the term is most common in English-language sources, although that means mixing both of these systems together. Below is a list of the key terms introduced in this chapter, in the order they appear, with spellings in both transcriptions as well as a brief note on proper pronunciation.

I-Ching / Yijing: Despite how nearly every Westerner mispronounces it, the proper pronunciation is "yee jing," not "eye ching."

Taoism / Daoism: No matter how it is written, this word should always be pronounced with an initial D instead of a T.

Tao / Dao: Also always pronounced with a D, as in "Dow Jones."

Tao Te Ching / Daode jing: Properly pronounced with two Ds and a J, not two Ts and a CH.

Laozi / Lao Tzu: This name is also sometimes spelled "Lao Tze." Whatever the spelling, it is pronounced "Lao-zz" with a long Z, not "Lao Zoo" or "Lao Zee."

Qi / Ch'i: Pronounced "chee." In transcriptions from the Japanese language, this is written *ki* and properly pronounced "kee."

Yin-yang: Say the A like you do in "father." Also, check that you're not making the mistake of saying "ying-yang."

Kung fu / Gongfu: Should be properly pronounced with a G instead of K. (Yes, you read that correctly!)

Tai-chi / Taiji: Properly pronounced with a J instead of a CH.

Qigong / Ch'i-kung: It includes the words *qi* and *gong* as in *gongfu* from above, so it's properly pronounced "chee gong."

Zhuangzi / Chuang Tzu: Properly pronounced "Jwong-zz," again with the long Z.

Perhaps you won't be surprised that this philosophy did not win any converts among the kings of the day, who preferred to continue to vie for power and make war with their neighbors. However, these ideas did get written down in a book that became enormously influential throughout the rest of Chinese history. That book was the *Tao Te Ching* (also spelled *Daode jing*) written by Lao Tzu (also spelled Laozi or Lao Tze). That name simply means "the Old Master," and not much is known about this author beyond legend. But his book became one of the most widely read philosophical treatises in China and, eventually, the world.

While Lao Tzu's pacifist model was not adopted by any Chinese government, the text and its author inspired a series of major religious movements in China about five centuries after it was written. Beginning in 142 CE and continuing today, many different religious groups have emerged in China that describe themselves as the embodiment of the *Tao Te Ching*'s teachings. The leaders of such groups also often have claimed to be able to channel or communicate spiritually with Lao Tzu. Collectively, these groups are often referred to as "religious Taoism," to differentiate them from the "philosophical Taoism" of the BCE period.

The sects of religious Taoism that have arisen throughout Chinese history have been diverse. But what they all have in common is that they have drawn ideas and practices from the same well of indigenous Chinese religions, medicine, and folkways, and then have systematized these to create formal models of religious practice. Many of these schools of religious Taoism were also heavily influenced by Buddhism, which was extremely popular in China. However, these schools all incorporated a wide range of meditation and visualization techniques, rituals, deities, movement-based practices, and other techniques that are uniquely Chinese. Chinese medicine and martial arts also draw from this same cultural well. Thus, there are similarities between them and Taoism, not because Chinese medicine and martial arts are Taoist but rather because these fields all incorporate the same indigenous Chinese ideas and practices.

Some of the most fundamental concepts in Chinese culture that are foundational to Taoism, medicine, and martial arts alike are *qi* and *yin-yang*. Qi (also spelled ch'i) appears across Chinese culture in countless contexts. This word is used to articulate ideas not only in the fields of Taoism, traditional medicine, and martial arts but also in politics, cosmology, aesthetics, astrology, and many other arenas of knowledge. Across all of these domains, you might say that qi points to dynamism and movement. It refers to aliveness, flow, and change. Qi can manifest in concrete, tangible ways, such as wind, the heat of the sun, or the sensations of the human body. Or it can be inscrutable, such as that energy that animates living beings or that makes the universe hum.

Yin-yang is another broad and encompassing concept that likewise crosses the boundaries of many disciplines and arts in Chinese culture. Essentially, yin-yang points at the harmonization of opposites or the resolution of dualities. Take any duality you can possibly think of (up vs. down, male vs. female, dark vs. light, and so forth). The theory of yin-yang says that you cannot have one without the other. For example, as soon as you speak of something being hot, you necessarily give birth to its opposite concept of cold. These polarities are mutually inseparable. In a way that's not entirely dissimilar from Hindu and Buddhist philosophy, the theory of yin-yang says that everything is nondual or interdependent.

Traditional Chinese healing systems are sophisticated sets of theories and practices about optimizing qi and yin-yang in the human body. For example, the system of healing commonly called in English "traditional Chinese medicine" was first articulated in the first century BCE in a book called the *Inner Canon of the Yellow Emperor*. This composition, which was attributed to the mythological emperor-god Huangdi, brought together for the first time the ideas of qi and yin-yang with the practice of acupuncture needling and a map of "meridian" channels of qi within the human body. All of these ingredients had emerged independently over the last few centuries BCE, but once they were brought together in the *Inner*

Canon, they became the basis of Chinese medical practice, as they continue to be to this day.

The two concepts of qi and yin-yang are also foundational to the practice of both Chinese martial arts and related movement-based therapies. Whether one is using movement to defeat an enemy or to help a patient, it is essential to understand the flows of qi and the dance of yin-yang within the physical body in order to maximize them and harness them for good use.

As martial arts have largely been transmitted through oral instruction and physical demonstration, there is not a huge amount of documentation on exactly how it was practiced. However, historical references go back to the last few centuries BCE. Martial arts have long had a close connection with religion in China. For example, the Shaolin monastery, a Buddhist temple in Henan province, has been a renowned center for martial arts since the sixth century CE. The most generic term that refers to the widest range of styles and approaches to martial arts is *kung fu* (also written *gongfu*). The purpose of kung fu, essentially, is to weaponize one's qi, to harness it through specialized movements and techniques so that it can be used to defeat an enemy or make oneself impermeable to attack.

The origins of movement-based therapies also date back quite far. The earliest physical exercise chart in the world was buried in a tomb at Mawangdui in Hunan province in 168 BCE. This chart depicts the practice of *daoyin*, an early movement-based health practice that was part of a whole cluster of diet, massage, sexual, and other self-cultivation techniques referred to as "nourishing life." Contemporary forms of therapeutic movement include *tai-chi* (also spelled *taiji*) and *qigong* (also spelled *ch'i kung*), both of which share some similarities with daoyin and certain kung fu methods.

All of the traditions mentioned in this section were popular throughout Chinese history and branched into many schools and styles of practice. Additionally, because China was for millennia the major power in East Asia, many aspects of Chinese civilization were imported and adopted by its neighbors. The ideas introduced here have therefore also had an enormous impact in Japan, Korea,

Taiwan, Vietnam, Mongolia, Tibet, and in Chinese-majority communities elsewhere in Asia. In all of those places, further adaptations and localizations took place that resulted in the development of locally specific forms of religious, medical, martial, and therapeutic practice. While here I have referred to these as "Chinese traditions" to emphasize their origins, it might be more accurate to refer to all of these as "East Asian" traditions, as they represent the shared heritage of the East Asian region.

Today, Western engagement with these East Asian spiritual traditions is a mixed bag. The *I-Ching* and *Tao Te Ching* have both been translated into English many times and now definitely qualify as two of the core texts of Western spirituality (see my comments on these translations in chapter 8). Another famous Taoist classic, the *Zhuangzi* (also written *Chuang Tzu*), written by Zhuang Zhou (369–286 BCE), is also a popular read among contemporary spiritual seekers. *The Art of War*, a manifesto on how to properly engage an enemy, written by Sun Wu (544–496 BCE), is not technically Taoist but expresses similar ideas. This book has become something of a cult classic in the modern West, particularly among armchair military theorists and aspiring business students. Nevertheless, while the philosophies expressed in all four of these books have had wide circulation in the West, there are extremely few Westerners who have gotten deeply involved with religious Taoism.

Martial arts are, of course, even more popular in the West than Taoism. Millions of Westerners, many of them children, participate in practicing karate, judo, jujitsu, tae kwon do, and other East Asian systems of martial arts every day. While most of these people probably see themselves as engaging in a sport or in learning self-defense, no doubt some percentage also see it as a spiritual practice. Certainly, Bruce Lee (1940–1973), the much-beloved Chinese American kung fu film star, philosopher, and poet, is often quoted as an authority in Western spiritual circles. Students of gentler movement practices associated with health and healing rather than fighting—such as tai chi, qigong, and related systems—are even more likely to think of their practice in spiritual terms.

BOX 2.4: *Tao Te Ching*, **Chapter 1**

Translated by A. Charles Muller (acmuller.net), with my edits.

The opening two lines from Lao Tzu's Tao Te Ching *are among the most famous lines in all of Chinese literature, known by heart by any educated person (the English equivalent perhaps would be "To be or not to be . . . " from Shakespeare's* Hamlet*). In this chapter, the fundamentally mysterious nonduality of the absolute truth (the nameless Tao) and all of its manifestations in the world (the myriad things) is laid out:*

> The Tao that can be spoken is not the eternal Tao.
> The name that can be named is not the eternal name.
> The nameless is the origin of heaven and earth,
> While naming is the origin of the myriad things.
> Therefore, always desireless, you see the mystery.
> Ever desiring, you see the manifestations.
> These two are the same—
> When they appear they are named differently.
> This sameness is the mystery,
> Mystery within mystery;
> The door to all marvels.

The practice of traditional Chinese medicine and other related East Asian healing arts (such as shiatsu and Reiki) can also be approached in two ways. While some practitioners are exclusively focused on the health benefits they can bring to themselves and their communities, others are interested in the spiritual value of the philosophies behind the medicine.

A QUICK NOTE ON WHAT'S NOT COVERED HERE

I hope you've enjoyed our whirlwind tour of Asian traditions. If it's a bit too much, don't worry—although I'm a college professor, there's no final exam at the end of this chapter! Before we finish this chapter giving you the lay of the land, I want to briefly mention some things that are not covered in this book.

One notable outcome of the meeting of Asian and Western cultures, which I discuss throughout this chapter, is the combination of Asian spirituality with all kinds of ingredients from Christianity, New Age, Western esotericism, paganism, and other forms of Western thought. Some of these novel practices originated in Asia and incorporated Western ideas (such as Pranic Healing and Won Buddhism, for example), while others are Western inventions that are to some extent riffing on Asian traditions (such as Tibetan singing-bowl therapy or "The Work" of Gurdjieff). There are also many practices that combine Asian spirituality with science, psychology, shamanism, hallucinogenic therapy, bodywork, energywork, and other forms of self-help, therapy, and self-improvement paradigms. Because there are so many of these hybrid systems, and because I don't want to get lost going off on too many tangents, I will not be discussing any of them in this book. That's not to say I don't like them or don't think they are worth learning. It's just that this book can only be so many pages long, and I've decided it's best to omit discussion of any hybrid systems in order to stay within a reasonable page count.

For the same reason, I will not be covering here practices that require years-long periods of formal training in order to learn. These include the practice of acupuncture, herbal medicine, and other specialized facets of Chinese, Tibetan, or Indian healing, all of which are tremendously complex and beyond what I can manage to include in this primer.

Finally, I will not be giving any detail here about practices that are traditionally kept secret within specific lineages. This includes popular practices such as Transcendental Meditation, as well as more esoteric ones such as Tibetan techniques requiring initiation empowerments. There are two interrelated reasons for this decision. First, as I am not initiated into any specific lineages, I don't feel I have any right to talk about these practices in public against the explicit wishes of the members of the tradition. I strongly believe that to do so would be an act of cultural appropriation.

Second, if it's required that you formally join a particular lineage before learning a technique, then by my definition that's no longer spiritual exploration. Once you cross the line into becoming an adherent of any particular system, you are going off the map of what's laid out in this book.

Again, I'm not passing judgment about any of the practices I'm not covering here; it's just that we have more than enough mileage to trek by simply focusing on the core traditions I've presented in this chapter.

———

Phew! That concludes our overview of the terrain. How are you feeling? We have just covered the basics, but even that is a lot to take in, isn't it? The landscape is huge when it's seen out the window of an airplane. Up here, at high altitude, the panoramic view is almost overwhelming.

You might be thinking, how can we even begin to explore this complex territory? With so many details to understand, where do we even start?

No worries, my fellow traveler. I know just the place to land this plane in order to start taking a closer look at things from the ground level. So, lace up your hiking boots! It's time to jump out and start exploring on foot!

BOX 2.5: Resources on the History of Asian Traditions

PRIMARY SOURCE TEXTS

- Wendy Doniger (ed.), *The Norton Anthology of World Religions: Hinduism*—A reliable collection of translations of the most influential passages from Hindu sacred texts
- Donald S. Lopez Jr. (ed.), *The Norton Anthology of World Religions: Buddhism*—A reliable collection of translations of the most influential passages from Buddhist sacred texts

- James Robson (ed.), *The Norton Anthology of World Religions: Daoism*—A reliable collection of translations of the most influential passages from Taoist sacred texts
- Thomas A. Tweed and Stephen Prothero (eds.), *Asian Religions in America: A Documentary History*—A collection of sources related to the history of Asian religions in the US

HISTORICAL STUDIES

- Livia Kohn, *Daoism and Chinese Culture*—An introduction to Taoism and its place in Chinese culture more generally
- Richard H. Robinson, Willard L. Johnson, and Thanissaro Bhikkhu, *Buddhist Religions: A Historical Introduction*—A detailed general introduction to the history of Buddhism
- Mark Singleton, *Yoga Body: The Origins of Modern Posture Practice*—A history of how yoga has transformed from a religious tradition to a health practice over the course of its history

CHAPTER 3

CORE PRACTICES FOR HEALTH AND WHOLENESS

Whatever circumstances have brought you here to the first steps of your journey into Asian spiritual traditions, this is a pivotal moment. Right now, you are standing at a crossroads that will define everything to come. The spiritual path begins with a fork in the road. One fork leads in the direction of what the Tibetan teacher Chögyam Trungpa pointedly called "spiritual materialism."

The vast majority of people who claim to be interested in Asian spirituality are actually walking on the path of spiritual materialism. They have co-opted spirituality, fitting it into the commercialism and superficiality of modern life. They treat spirituality like a trip to the shopping mall, seeking to acquire shiny new items that will burnish their image and self-esteem. They follow the trendiest guru, buy overpriced yoga pants from the "right" company, post Instagram photos from expensive retreats, and rebrand themselves as a "spiritual person."

Spiritual materialism is a dead-end path because it does not lead to results that are any different or any more fulfilling than regular materialism. However, there is another option here at the crossroads: the other fork, which leads in a completely different direction. Far fewer people are drawn to walk this way. There are no fancy bells and whistles to attract you, no trendy gear to buy or glossy magazines to read. There's not much here to feed your ego either or to use in fashioning a new, trendier identity. This path is not about making yourself look like a healthy and whole person on social media; it's about authentically taking steps toward actually becoming one.

The Asian spiritual traditions are unanimous in saying that, ultimately, true fulfillment cannot be found in ordinary, day-to-day human social life. It sounds clichéd, but true fulfillment can only be found within. Thus, an authentic spiritual path presents a big hurdle right from the get-go. It starts with having to embrace an uncomfortable truth: Before you can even take one step, you have to acknowledge those feelings of longing and unfulfillment you have been feeling. You have to be honest with yourself, and actually feel your feelings instead of trying to hide them behind consumerism and image.

So, ask yourself, are you ready to turn within with honesty and authenticity? If you are indeed ready to start on a process of self-transformation, then this chapter will get you outfitted with the basic equipment you need to begin. Here you will find four simple adaptations of traditional Asian practices that provide accessible starting points to true self-transformation. They will be the core practices of your journey of health and wellness, and the foundation for everything to come later in the book.

MINDFULNESS

The Buddha talked about that feeling of longing and unfulfillment I discussed just a moment ago using the Pali word *dukkha*. He made overcoming dukkha the core idea of his whole system of teaching. As we have seen, Buddhism is a hugely complicated tradition with many schools and sub-schools. However, there is one commonly taught practice to alleviate dukkha that is shared across nearly the whole spectrum of Buddhism. That key practice is mindfulness.

Mindfulness is usually recommended to all beginning practitioners of Buddhism. It is also a practice the Buddha highly praised as an advanced tool for achieving enlightenment. Fortunately for us modern Western spiritual explorers, mindfulness training is widely available today in countless formats and is consequently one of the easiest Asian spiritual techniques to learn. That being said, there are a few potential potholes on the path of mindfulness that I'll point out here, so be sure to skim this section even if you are already familiar with the practice.

First, let's define mindfulness. In essence, you can say that mindfulness is a kind of meditation, which in turn is a type of contemplative practice. Starting with the broadest category, a contemplative practice is any method of intentionally turning your attention inward. It's any technique that helps you to shift your focus from the goings-on of the day-to-day and instead pay attention to your own internal world. Some common contemplative practices include journaling, taking a pensive walk, and enjoying a moment of silent reflection. In general, Asian spiritual traditions recommend maximizing these kinds of activities throughout the day. If you are faced with the choice between mindlessly scrolling through your social media feed or vegging out on a TV show versus taking a hot bath, letting your body relax, and allowing your thoughts to unwind, you know which one I'm going to recommend.

The subcategory of contemplative practice that concerns us here is meditation. This word originates in the Latin term for certain kinds of Christian religious activities, but in mainstream English today it most often refers to practices taught by Asian spiritual traditions. Meditation can refer to chanting, prayer, reflection, visualization, or many other kinds of practice that Buddhist traditions teach. There are literally thousands of variations of meditation taught by Buddhist groups. The most well known in the West include the practices called *vipassana*, *jhana*, *zazen*, *metta*, and *dzogchen*, all of which I will discuss in future chapters.

Among all of these different practices, the English word *mindfulness* is the translation of the name of one specific kind of Buddhist meditation, called in Pali *sati*. The original meaning of this term is "to recollect," "to remember," or "to bear in mind." This practice is mentioned in countless texts throughout the Buddhist world, but if you're interested in reading some original sources, you might

Google the two Pali texts called *Anapanasati Sutta* (*Discourse on the Mindfulness of Breathing*) and *Satipatthana Sutta* (*Discourse on the Bases of Mindfulness*), both of which are readily available in English translation online. As described in these texts and others like them, the practice of sati involves attending to the present state of your own body and mind. (In other words, if you're meditating on a visualization, or listening to music, or chanting a mantra, or otherwise introducing an external meditation object, it's not actually mindfulness.)

Attending to the present state of your body and mind can mean bearing in mind the movements of your body, or the "feeling tone" of your body overall, or specific body sensations. Or it could mean paying attention to the mood or disposition of your mind more generally, or specific phenomena that appear in your mind, like thoughts, images, memories, and perceptions.

What exactly you're going to bear in mind, and how you're going to do it, varies across Buddhist traditions. However, by far the most common variation of mindfulness is meditating on the feeling of the breath going in and out of your body. Another popular option is to mentally sweep through the body in order to scan your body sensations. Yet another widespread option is called "open awareness," in which you pay attention to whatever aspect of your body or mind happens to be catching your attention in any given moment.

I'll give you some recommendations for practice later, but because we're spiritual explorers and not partisans of any particular school of Buddhism, I would recommend experimenting with several different styles of mindfulness and see which one works best for you. These days it's easy to find instructions for different approaches through books, YouTube, and smartphone apps. (Just don't fall for the marketing hype: if it's not encouraging you to calmly attend to your own body and mind, then it's not mindfulness!)

Whatever aspect of your body or mind is the object of your meditation, the idea with sati is to bear it in mind or remember it. But don't misunderstand this as meaning that the meditation object should completely absorb all of your attention. This is the single-most common error for beginning students of mindfulness. They imagine that they should sit, close their eyes, and pay full, uninterrupted attention to their breathing without any distraction for the whole time. When instead they find that their minds are constantly flitting around from place to place, they tell themselves "I'm doing it wrong," "I'm no good at this," or "Oh, well, I tried; I guess I'll give up." That is not mindfulness. In fact, it's the complete opposite of mindfulness. When learning this practice, it is imperative to stay neutral and nonjudgmental, and not spin out into self-criticism and doubt.

It will be extremely helpful if you keep in mind that *sati* means "remembering," not "concentrating." So, if you did mindfulness of breathing for a period of time and were super distracted, but you periodically remembered to notice your breathing, then you actually did a lot of mindfulness. Each time you remembered to return to the breath was a moment of mindfulness. As you devote yourself to practicing more over time, you might find the number of these moments of mindfulness you experience increasing. But being fully absorbed in your breath without any fluctuation is not the goal here. (There are practices in which full concentration is the goal, and I'll introduce those in the next chapter, but that's not what we're talking about here.)

So, let's talk a bit about why I'm including this practice here in this chapter about the most important Asian spiritual practices for health and wholeness. I have already mentioned that this core Buddhist practice is shared by almost all the schools and sub-schools that developed worldwide, so surely it must have some benefits, right? Well, indeed it does! Buddhist teachers are quick to point out that one of the best benefits of mindfulness is that it helps us to break out of mind-wandering and mental rumination (in Pali called *papancha*). Each time you bring your attention back to the object of your meditation, you train yourself to let go of this habit.

These claims, made by the Buddhist tradition over two thousand years ago, have now been amply confirmed by modern scientists. Mindfulness is, in fact, the most well-researched practice of all the Asian spiritual traditions. (I mentioned earlier that there are currently over 8,500 scientific articles with the word *mindfulness* in their titles listed in PubMed.org, the authoritative research database maintained by the US National Institutes of Health.) I usually don't talk too much about science when it comes to Asian spirituality, but I think it's worth exploring these findings for just a moment.

Scientists researching mindfulness have found that one of its chief benefits is to disrupt the activity of a process in the brain called the "default mode network." The DMN is active when your brain is not focused on anything in particular. Have you ever been walking down the street, driving a car, or taking a shower and realized that you've been on autopilot while your mind has been wandering off on a journey of its own? Of course you have; everyone has! Whenever you're not giving your brain another task to concentrate on, your DMN flips on and starts chattering about your to-do list, your memories, what you like and don't like, what you might like to eat for lunch, and all sorts of other random things. These wandering thoughts often are harmless, but for many, they can be relentlessly self-critical, emotionally triggering, and anxiety producing.

By doing mindfulness you are gradually training your brain to short-circuit the DMN, to release the habit of ruminating on this critical self-talk, and instead return to paying attention to what's actually going on in the moment. According to the research, this disruption of the DMN is so beneficial that even doing ten to fifteen minutes of mindfulness per day has a measurably positive effect on your mental health. In essence, the less you allow the DMN to chatter on, the happier you become. And because the relentless rumination of the DMN is directly linked to mental illnesses like anxiety and depression, mindfulness has become a mainstream treatment for these kinds of conditions and many other mental health concerns as well.

These days not only is mindfulness used routinely by therapists for all sorts of patients; it also has found a place within Western school systems to help students concentrate better, elevate their test scores, and reduce behavioral problems. It has been introduced in prisons to lessen inmate violence and recidivism. It is being used in companies large and small in order to improve productivity and alleviate stress at work. And in a whole number of other contexts across Western society, mindfulness is being used to improve quality of life and increase happiness.

Now, I really think it's wonderful that mindfulness can bring so many benefits to so many people in so many settings. But I also think that the runaway popularity of mindfulness should also make us pause and look a bit more closely at the practice. Remember Chögyam Trungpa's warning about spiritual materialism? Well, a company using mindfulness to enhance the productivity of the workforce is just about the clearest example of spiritual materialism I can think of. Is that really what the Buddha envisioned when he taught his fellow monks to practice sati? Do you think he would condone the mindfulness products, magazines, and costly trainings that now add up to a two-billion-dollar-a-year industry in the US, according to MarketResearch.com?

The question of materialism aside, there are other dark implications of the mindfulness craze. For example, if a company uses mindfulness to reduce employees' stress at work, does that mean the owners don't actually have to take responsibility for the fact that it's a stressful workplace? If prisons use mindfulness to improve prisoner relations, are they distracting from the fact that the prison system itself is dehumanizing? If schools use mindfulness to help children concentrate better on their work, does it occur to anyone to question whether it's right to force children to sit at desks for so many hours per day in the first place?

As spiritual explorers, we aren't just going to go with the crowd. We have the obligation to investigate, analyze, and understand the use and misuse of any of the practices we are embracing. We need to be able to see clearly how these practices can affect our lives without romanticizing them or wearing blinders that help us to ignore their potential downsides. (For more on such critical perspectives, see chapter 8.)

BOX 3.1: Introductory Mindfulness
of Breathing Practice

Follow the basic instructions here, or feel free to find a guided mindfulness record-ing that you prefer on YouTube or one of the meditation apps (my current favorite recommendation is the fifty-day introductory program on the Waking Up app). Be discerning about which recording you choose and prioritize any preferences you have as to the gender, tone of voice, and terminology used by the guide. If you don't use a guided meditation, you should still get yourself a simple meditation timer app or a nice ringtone for your smartphone's built-in timer.

Pick a specific time that's going to work for you on a daily basis and commit to practicing daily. If fifteen minutes seems too long, you can start with as little as two minutes and build up gradually. If you feel like you can do more, you can extend up to forty or even sixty minutes, either all at once or split into two daily sessions. What's most important at first is to establish consistency, so instead of trying to practice for as long as possible, set up a schedule that you will be able to stick with for the long term.

When it's time to practice, do so in a quiet space with minimal distractions. Sit comfortably. For the practice of mindfulness, there's no reason to sit in any particular posture. You can even lie down and do it in bed if you find that it helps you to fall asleep!

Although it's not required, most people find when starting out that they can be more mindful if they close their eyes. Eventually, you'll be able to practice in the midst of a noisy, chaotic environment with your eyes wide open. But, for now, take it easy on yourself and block out some of the visual distractions.

Once you are settled, discover a place on your body where you can distinctly feel your breath in the form of a body sensation. This could be the sensation of the rise and fall of your abdomen, the inflation and deflation of your chest, or the air moving in and out of your throat or nostrils. It does not matter what spot you choose, but the clearer the sensation, the easier it will be to be mindful of it.

Now, rest your mind in the sensations of breathing. Remember that it's not about clinging to the object of mindfulness, so don't try to grab on to it. Just let your attention gently float along with the body sensations.

Your default mode network will inevitably kick in, and you'll find yourself daydreaming, mind-wandering, ruminating, planning for the future, revisiting past events, and so forth. No problem! This might happen hundreds or thousands of times per session. But each time, you'll eventually remember to come back and rest in the sensations of your breath. Each time that happens, you've experienced one more moment of mindfulness.

To repeat what I said earlier, please don't criticize yourself or get frustrated that your mind wanders. We are not here to cultivate more stress and self-loathing! Remember that wandering is precisely what your brain is designed to do when it's not involved in any specific task. When you catch it doing so, just smile and gently come back to resting in the object. This short-circuits the DMN, while worrying about not being good at meditation will just feed it.

Once your timer goes off to finish your session, go about the rest of your life normally. During the day, you may find yourself having a spontaneous moment or two of mindfulness where your attention returns to the breath, even when you're in the middle of doing something else. If so, enjoy these bonus mindful moments!

In light of all of this, and in line with my previous comments on spiritual materialism, my suggestion is that you do not take up the practice of mindfulness in order to gain any specific tangible benefits in the day-to-day world. Definitely don't make it about getting new meditation gear so you can post about it on social media. But, by extension, don't make it about increasing your productivity at work, lowering your stress, or bettering your concentration either. Or about enhancing your sex life, or managing your weight, or better fulfilling your life goals.

Instead, make the sole purpose of your effort simply to enhance your health, wholeness, and spiritual growth in general. You definitely will see other benefits from your practice, I promise, but let those arise naturally instead of turning them into an explicit agenda. Things will take time—think in terms of months or years, not days—but, gradually, you'll see positive outcomes in your life.

GROUNDING

Mindfulness is your core tool for dealing with the critical self-talk and other chatter that's cluttering up your mental space. In this section, we are going to acquire a second practice that will do something similar for your body.

Just as your mind is constantly acting out the habits it has accumulated, your body is doing so as well. These unconscious bodily habits include, for example, clenching your jaw, fidgeting with your thumb and forefinger, chewing your nails or cuticles, or any number of other tics and quirks. All of these patterns—which everyone experiences—are indicative of residual tension and stress in the physical body.

This background stress is exacerbated by the anxieties we experience throughout the day. These range from major stressors (such as a collision on the way to work or an argument with a coworker once you got there) to minor ones (such as accidentally biting the inside of your cheek when eating dinner or your momentary annoyance at your dogs for barking at the mailman). Even more subtle micro-stressors, which are so small you may not even realize they are bothering you, still pile up over time. These might include the slight jolt you get from your alarm going off in the morning or the barely perceptible twinge of anxiety you feel when your phone's notification sound goes off.

Most of us living in the fast-paced modern world go through our day with thousands of stressors like this bombarding our bodies at every moment. We may occasionally try to relax in order to take a break from it all. But most of the time, we seem to be making things worse instead. We stay up too late, we jack ourselves up on caffeine, we run late for meetings, we don't eat well, we eat too much or not enough. All day long, we pile stress upon stress, and we just expect our bodies to absorb all of this without complaining. Meanwhile, our bodies are desperately trying to process all the chaos being thrown their way. Inevitably, they can do so successfully for only so long, and it's only a matter of time till your body crashes into exhaustion, fatigue, and even physical illness.

In the same way that we needed to find a practice to help us more skillfully relate to our minds, we also need to find a practice that will help us to befriend our bodies. We need a way to get out of this boom-and-bust cycle of jacking up and crashing down, to help us to more harmoniously regulate ourselves and achieve better balance. In this section, I will introduce two introductory practices that will help us to do just that. They are called "grounding practices," in the sense that they utilize the ground—actually, technically, they use gravity—as a way of bringing us back into a healthier relationship with our bodies.

While we drew mindfulness from Buddhism in the previous section, here, we are going to introduce practices that come from Hindu and Chinese traditions. Importantly, both of these spiritual systems understand the human body to be more than just its physical material structure. They also speak about the energetic component of the body. I talked about the Chinese notion of qi in the previous chapter, and there's a largely analogous concept in the yoga traditions called *prana*. We'll get deeper into this topic in chapter 6. For the moment, let's just say that talking about "energy" means talking about the overall feeling tone of your body, the felt sense of what it's like to be inside your body.

In modern medical terms, this internal sense of your body is known as interoception. So, when I say that the practices introduced next will help you to tune in to your energy body, what I mean is that they will help hone your interoception, to make your internal perception a more accessible part of your awareness.

To illustrate what I mean, direct your attention into your body, not focusing on any one specific sensation but feeling the overall sense of what's going on in there right now. Do your body sensations feel generally unsettled, scattered, or airy, like your body is the wind blowing in all directions at once? Or maybe do they feel heavy, slow, or tired, like your body is a clump of sticky mud? Or do they feel some other way altogether? Tuning in like this while doing grounding practices can be really helpful. These techniques combine interoception, relaxation, and breathing in order to rapidly and efficiently reset your whole energy field. You'll know the exercises are working when you feel comfortable, solid, and relaxed—but also awake and aware instead of sleepy or lethargic.

In boxes 3.2 and 3.3, I'm presenting you with two options for grounding. Try them both for a couple of days and see which one you like best. Once you've made your selection, then practice that technique daily for ten to fifteen minutes. When you do so is up to you. Perhaps it makes the most sense to do this at the end of the workday, in order to unwind and let go of the busyness of your job. Or maybe you find that doing it right before bed helps you to sleep better. Or you might find it convenient to do it just before or after your mindfulness practice. Find the time that works best for you, and try to stick to a regular schedule. (As I talked about in the previous section, consistency really helps to ingrain a new habit.)

BOX 3.2: Basic Grounding Practice 1

CORPSE POSE BELLY BREATHING (SHAVASANA)

Some variation of this grounding practice is normally used at the end of most Western yoga classes.

Find a quiet place where you will not be interrupted. For comfort, you may wish to place a blanket, rug, or yoga mat under your body.

Lay yourself on your back, flat on the ground, with your legs slightly apart and your arms away from your body. Experiment with what's most comfortable; the goal should be to maximize the relaxation of your whole body.

Feel the curvature of your spine against the ground. For most people, there will be a point of contact on the back of the head, then an arch at your neck, a point of contact in the middle of your back, then an arch at your lower back, and finally a point of contact at your sacrum. If lying in this way this makes you feel at all uncomfortable, you can bend your knees to remove the arch at your lower back. Or you can lie on your side. Use bolsters or pillows to prop up your legs so that you can totally relax them.

Once you are comfortably in your posture, take a moment to feel yourself embraced by gravity and fully resting against the ground.

When you are ready, begin to belly breathe. Draw a slow and deep breath in through your nostrils, extending your belly as if it's inflating with air like a balloon. When your belly is fully extended, keep drawing the breath into your lungs, expanding your chest. When your lungs are completely full, keep drawing the breath into the area underneath your collarbones at the base of your neck. When all of the space in your abdomen is completely full with air, hold your breath for a moment. Pause here to feel the sensation of fullness throughout your body as it rests on the ground.

Now release, allowing all the air to slowly and effortlessly flow out of your nostrils. Relax your abdomen, diaphragm, chest, and collarbones, allowing everything to return to the embrace of gravity. When the entire breath has been exhaled, pause for a moment and feel the stillness before the next breath.

That completes one cycle. Repeat for ten to fifteen minutes, or longer if you wish.

A common variation is to use a breathing pattern called "coherent breathing." This involves timing your inhalations and exhalations for about five seconds each. (There are lots of timers online that can help to keep you on track, or just count in your head.) Another common variation is "box breathing." This involves breathing in, holding, breathing out, and holding for an even amount of time. (There is no prescribed amount of time, so just count in order to maintain equal intervals.)

Coherent breathing and box breathing are two of the most effective ways to use breathing to calm down a hyper-aroused nervous system, and both have been researched for medical and therapeutic applications. Both methods have similarities with the yogic breathing exercises called *pranayama*. Because true pranayama is a more advanced technique with unpredictable results, it is best to start with these two simple, safe, and effective breathing patterns instead.

BOX 3.3: Basic Grounding Practice 2

POST STANCE (ZHANZHUANG)

This grounding practice originally comes from the Chinese practices of qigong, tai chi, and martial arts.

Find a quiet place where you will not be interrupted. Remove your shoes. If there is no carpet, you may wish to place a towel, yoga mat, or small rug under your feet for comfort.

Begin by standing with your feet shoulder-width apart or slightly wider. Plant each foot solidly on the ground by making a little tripod between your heel, the ball of your big toe, and the ball of your fourth toe. Your weight should be distributed evenly between each of these points. For most of you, your feet will be more or less parallel, pointing in front of you.

(continues)

Bending your knees, sink down into your hips like you are trying to lower your perineum to place it directly between your feet. Don't bend your knees any more forward than your toes. Rest your arms at the side of your body, with your palms facing inward at each other, and relax everything from your shoulders down to your fingertips. Feel your feet solidly connecting with the ground and the weight of your legs, arms, and whole body resting on the earth.

Without adjusting your solid base, feel your spine growing tall, rising upward from your sacrum to the top of your head. With your chin gently tucked in, balance your head directly on top of your spine, neither too far forward nor behind. It may help to picture a buoy chained to the bottom of a lake. The links in the chain are pulled into a straight line by the buoy, which floats weightlessly on the surface of the water. Feel the upward lift along each vertebra of your spine, from your anchored sacrum up to your weightless head.

Touch your tongue to your palate, rest your gaze or close your eyes, and begin to belly breathe in this position (see exercise 3.2 for belly-breathing instructions). With each exhalation, sink your center of gravity more deeply into the earth. With each inhalation, feel your head becoming more and more buoyant. Feel the sensations of these deep waves of breath moving through a body that is simultaneously planted firmly on the ground while also floating in space.

Some schools of qigong advocate standing like this for hours at a time. However, it is very likely that, when first starting out, your legs will fatigue rapidly and start shaking uncontrollably. Unless you have unusually strong legs, you probably will need to start with shorter time periods, like three to five minutes, and build up over time to about ten to fifteen minutes.

In addition to the main practice time, you can also throw in an extra few minutes here and there as needed throughout the day. Did you just have a difficult interaction with someone? A traumatic memory got triggered? A close call while driving? Drop into your grounding practice and see how quickly it can help to settle your physical signs of stress (breathing rate, heart rate, etc.) as well as your energetic ones (feeling unsettled, scattered, etc.).

Over time, you will find that these practices start kicking in automatically, helping your body to recover its equilibrium whenever you get agitated, stressed, or emotionally upset. In time, you'll find that all you have to do is orient your awareness in a certain way while you exhale and your whole being will instantly feel grounded. Conversely, whenever you feel run down or sluggish, you will see that your body feels more refreshed by ten to fifteen minutes of grounding than it does when you gulp down yet another cup of coffee or eat a sugary sweet in an attempt to keep your energy up.

Think of your grounding practice as an "energetic first-aid kit" that you can pull out any time a stress response is invoked in your body. Even if you can't do the whole exercise in that moment, just doing the interoceptive feeling and the belly-breathing parts of it can work wonders. While there is far less empirical research on these particular grounding practices than there is for mindfulness, PubMed does list some studies that show these techniques can lead to reduced stress, improvements in cardiovascular health (notably blood pressure and heart rate variability), and improvements in autonomic balance. That being said, I don't think you'll need to read medical studies in order to convince yourself that you feel better when you are grounded!

Beyond how these practices help you manage the day-to-day ups and downs, their true magic is how they help you to more fully inhabit your body in the long term. Over time, you will feel more present and more aware of your interoception. You will also become more and more receptive to receiving messages from this level of your being, more readily accessing your body's deeper wisdom. Again, think in terms of months or years, but eventually, you will see that this process of tuning in is repairing the alienation and tension between yourself and your body. And this is absolutely central to becoming more healthy and whole.

TAKING CARE

Mindfulness and grounding are two of the most important basic practices of spiritual cultivation, focusing on your mind and your energy body, respectively. Equally important to taking care of yourself, however, is cultivating positive and healthy relationships with all of the other beings around you. It's simply impossible to experience wholeness if you are out of balance with your community, your environment, and your world.

There are many tools we could draw from Asian spiritual traditions to help us to more skillfully connect with others, and I'll introduce several in chapter 4. However, in my opinion, the single most potent and far-reaching concept to use as a starting point is *ahimsa*. Ahimsa is multifaceted, so I will unpack it here in successive layers. At the most elementary level, the literal translation of the term is "nonviolence."

Ahimsa is enshrined as the first of the ethical guidelines (*yamas*) in the *Yoga Sutras*, which makes it the very first step of the traditional practice of yoga. Likewise, it is the first of the fundamental vows in the ancient Indian religion of Jainism, and a closely related term is the first of the moral precepts of Buddhism. In other words, what these Indian traditions agree on is that refraining from acts of violence is the very first step on the spiritual path. In fact, a great deal of the other ethical rules or precepts that these traditions prescribe truly are just elaborations on this primary moral principle.

I imagine that most readers of this book probably would agree that it is important not to commit acts of abject violence toward other beings. But you should pause to consider the extent to which this ethical commitment is adhered to by practitioners in India. Some ardent followers of Jainism, for example, sweep the ground in front of them as they walk in order to remove insects they might happen to step on. Some Jain sects require wearing screens over your mouth and nose in case you happen to inadvertently breathe in any living beings.

Most Jains are completely vegetarian, as are most Hindus and many Buddhists as well. That is to say, their concern for ahimsa extends not only to avoiding acts of violence toward animals themselves but also refraining from supporting the killing of animals by others. To take on board the concept of ahimsa is to think not only about the consequences of your own direct actions but about what kinds of actions you are willing to support indirectly as well.

In modern times, practitioners of these traditions have expanded the concept of ahimsa even further. Many have noted, for example, how our modern lifestyles contribute to the death of not just animals but also plant life and, indeed, entire ecosystems. For example, I may not be wielding a harpoon and killing whales myself, but have I considered how the plastics that I throw in the trash every day wind up in the ocean, contributing to the decimation of plankton, the de-oxygenation of the water, and the death of all kinds of marine life? Have I considered the broader environmental effects of my choice in food, cars, clothing, and other products? Have I truly taken in the magnitude of the global ecological crisis and taken clear responsibility for my own part in that catastrophe? The practice of ahimsa requires clear seeing and self-honesty to not to look away from the consequences of my actions, no matter how uncomfortable that may be for me.

Before you get the wrong idea, though, I am not arguing that everyone needs to run out right now and become vegan and swear off plastic for life. All-or-nothing thinking like that is, in fact, detrimental to spirituality! The point I am making here is that ahimsa belongs in your gear bag as one of the core values of an ethically sensitive life. Use the concept of ahimsa to analyze your actions and their consequences starting wherever you are today, and then continue to employ this self-reflection on an ongoing basis moving forward throughout your life. Continually ask yourself "How are my actions harming other beings?" and gradually try to minimize that harm wherever and whenever you can.

If you approach ahimsa as a lifelong practice, you will find over time that this tool is working for you in more and more subtle ways. You might graduate beyond simply minimizing physical harm to other beings, extending the notion of ahimsa to more intangible kinds of violence. Consider verbal harm, for example. The *Yoga Sutras*, Jainism, and Buddhism all consider truthfulness to be a core value. Buddhism specifically advocates "right speech," teaching practitioners to avoid divisive or abusive words, as well as idle gossip. Applying the lens of ahimsa to the realm of speech might initially mean refraining from talking behind people's backs at the office and avoiding arguing politics on social media. At a more subtle level, you might investigate your habitual tendency to subtly undermine other people or to paint them in a less positive light than you could.

I am giving examples of how the practice of ahimsa might bring to light certain ways that you are inadvertently harming others. Ahimsa is a tool for reflection that can help you to recognize where you have been unconscious about the impact of your behavior on other beings. Once you see where you have been unconscious, you can choose to act more consciously. (Of course, sometimes you may not have a real choice, and sometimes violence is unavoidable; even the Jains allow for acts of violence in self-defense.) In this way, the Indian traditions take us through a process of spiritual development that starts with ethical dos and don'ts and gradually leads to deeper and deeper internal transformations.

The internalization of ahimsa at the deepest level leads eventually to us becoming a friend to all beings. A person who exhibits universal friendliness (Sanskrit *maitri*) walks gently in the world. They take care of others out of a natural overflowing of their compassion. They literally could not bring themselves to hurt a fly. Indian traditions agree that genuinely embodying universal friendliness is a marker of a highly evolved spiritual person. In certain traditions, it may be the largest component or even the only requirement for enlightenment.

Having written all of that, I'm afraid that some readers will start to get down on themselves after reading this section. Please keep in mind that ahimsa is not a tool for blaming and shaming yourself. The point of ahimsa is not to chastise you for being an imperfect person or compel you to hold unreasonable expectations over your head. These are not black-and-white commandments but rather points of self-reflection. So, if you are pressuring yourself or being self-critical, please let go of that rumination. Being a friend to the world starts with being a friend to yourself. Practicing right speech begins with right speech toward yourself, inside your own head.

Asian approaches to spirituality are not asking us to be perfect in every way right out of the box. Nor are they asking us to take on the burdens of the whole world and to try to fix everything overnight. What is being asked of us is to start wherever we are, and to take whatever steps we can, one at a time, over the long term, in order to gradually transform ourselves in positive ways. So, start with a micro-dose of ahimsa today—whether it's being kind to someone else or to yourself—and trust that this practice, over time, will supercharge your journey of healing and wholeness.

BOX 3.4: Excerpt from the *Discourse on Universal Friendliness (Karaniya Metta Sutta)*

Translated by Peter Harvey in *An Introduction to Buddhism: Teachings, History and Practices* (Cambridge University Press, 2013), with my edits.

This excerpt of a short text from the Pali collection of Buddhist scriptures is a powerful call to be a friend to all beings. In a portion not quoted here, the text says that someone who sustains this "divine meditation" will achieve liberation.

May all beings be happy and secure, may they be happy-minded! Whatever living beings there are—feeble or strong, long, stout or medium, short, small or large, seen or unseen [i.e., ghosts, gods and hell-beings], those dwelling far or near, those who are born or those who await rebirth—may all beings, without exception, be happy-minded! Let none deceive another nor despise any person whatever in any place; in anger or ill will let them not wish any suffering to each other. Just as a mother would protect her only child at the risk of her own life, even so, let the practitioner cultivate a boundless heart towards all beings.

Let their thoughts of boundless lovingkindness pervade the whole world: above, below and across, without obstruction, without any hatred, without any enmity.

Whether they stand, walk, sit, or lie down, as long as they are awake, they should develop this mindset. This, they say, is divine abiding. . . .

LETTING GO AND FINDING FLOW

The fourth and final core practice I'll introduce in this chapter is letting go of what isn't working for you and finding the natural flow of your life. Different traditions speak of the importance of letting go in different terms, depending on their target audience and their intended outcomes. Many forms of Hinduism, for example, advocate letting go of being enmeshed in worldly things by cultivating an attitude of detachment toward wealth, occupation, and social status. Buddhism agrees with this and typically encourages people to follow the Buddha's example by giving up one's worldly life, giving up one's possessions, and going to live the simple life of an ascetic monk or nun.

Letting go of wealth and status in order to live a simple and uncomplicated life is also central to Taoism's philosophy of non-action or non-doing (*wuwei*). One of the most famous illustrations of this principle is a story about the sage Zhuang Zhou, nicknamed Zhuangzi. This story appears in the book that bears Zhuangzi's name (see an excerpt in box 3.5). Once, the master was visited by high officials who came at the king's bidding in order to offer him a prestigious job at court. Zhuangzi turned them down by drawing an analogy between himself and a holy tortoise. The moral of the story is that the sage would much prefer to live unencumbered by worldly things rather than trade in that freedom for even the highest prestige, honor, and wealth.

Aside from embracing letting go of the world, Asian traditions also urge us to let go of control. The epic Hindu poem the *Bhagavad Gita* teaches that we should always do what is right and just, without being attached to any of the "fruits," or the outcomes, of our actions. Taoist teachings similarly advocate surrendering to the Tao, the flow of life, and allowing it to carry us in whatever direction is natural in that moment. To be clear: this does not mean simply being passive, or letting people walk all over you. Rather, it is surrendering one's desire to control what cannot be controlled, so that the actions one does take will effortlessly follow the path of least resistance.

Another famous story from the *Zhuangzi* illustrates this point vividly (also in box 3.5). In the parable of Carver Ding, a king gets a lesson in non-action from a skilled butcher. Although Ding is talking about carving up a bull, the king immediately recognizes the broader implications of his wisdom for all aspects of life. The king remarks that this way of life preserves one's "vital forces." And that's one of the main points I want to get across in this section. Surrendering to the path of least resistance allows you to stop wasting your energy, your bandwidth, and your vitality on things that are ultimately not important or not serving you. It allows you to conserve yourself for what truly brings you meaning, purpose, and joy.

BOX 3.5: Two stories from the Taoist classic *Zhuangzi*, by Zhuang Zhou

Translated by Arthur Waley in *Three Ways of Thought in Ancient China* (George Allen & Unwin, 1939), with my edits.

THE HOLY TORTOISE

When Zhuangzi was fishing in the river Pu, the king of Chu sent two high officers of state, who accosted Zhuangzi announcing that the king wished to entrust him with the management of all his domains.

Rod in hand and eyes still fixed upon his line, Zhuangzi replied, "I have been told that in Chu there is a holy tortoise that died three thousand years ago. The king keeps it in the great hall of his ancestral shrine, in a casket covered with a cloth.

"Suppose that when this tortoise was caught, it had been allowed to choose between dying and having its bones venerated for centuries to come or going on living with its tail draggling in the mud. Which would it have preferred?"

"No doubt," said the two officers, "it would have preferred to go on living with its tail draggling in the mud."

"Well then, be off with you," said Zhuangzi, "and leave me to drag my tail in the mud!"

CARVER DING

King Hui of Wei had a carver named Ding. When this carver Ding was carving a bull for the king, every touch of the hand, every inclination of the shoulder, every

(continues)

step he trod, every pressure of the knee, while swiftly and lightly he wielded his carving-knife, was as carefully timed as the movements of a dancer. . . .

"Wonderful," said the king. "I could never have believed that the art of carving could reach such a point as this."

"I am a lover of the Tao," replied Ding. putting away his knife, "and have succeeded in applying it to the art of carving. . . . Nowadays I no longer see [the bull] with the eye; I merely apprehend it with the soul. . . . Unerringly my knife follows the natural markings, slips into the natural cleavages, finds its way into the natural cavities. And so by conforming my work to the structure with which I am dealing, I have arrived at a point at which my knife never touches even the smallest ligament or tendon. . . .

"A good carver changes his knife once a year; by which time the blade is dented. An ordinary carver changes it once a month; by which time it is broken. I have used my present knife for nineteen years, and during that time have carved several thousand bulls. But the blade still looks as though it had just come out of the mold. . . .

"Excellent," said the king of Wei. "This interview with the carver Ding has taught me how one's vital forces can be conserved."

As you know, I'm a college professor, and in my line of work I see countless young people who could use Zhuangzi's advice. So many students are in college because they think they have to be. In fact, they may be better served by going to a trade school, traveling the world, starting a business, or any number of other things, but instead they are stuck in a rut just doing what they've been told they're supposed to do.

Even those students who really are a good fit for college often find themselves pursuing popular degrees like business, finance, premed, or computers because that's what their parents expect of them, when in fact they really may be personally better suited to majoring in the arts, philosophy, literature, or whatever. Because they are not flowing with the Tao and doing what comes naturally to them, they experience everything about college to be a struggle. Instead of dancing like Carver Ding, they find themselves constantly hacking away with a blunt knife.

Countless people continue this same pattern after graduation, heading into jobs that they are not passionate about and are not suited for because they have accepted what they've been told by society. Ignoring their inner calling, they tell themselves that they have to dedicate their life to making money, to being "productive citizens," and so forth. They may never pause to consider what other options there are, what their own true calling may be, or what their deepest self is longing to express in the world. The more they ignore the Tao calling out to them, the further away they get from happiness.

Symptoms of living this kind of unfulfilled life in conflict with one's own Tao include amassing material possessions and status symbols, false displays of happiness that are conformist and superficial, midlife crises and other patterns of self-sabotage, and trying to numb oneself with distractions and addictions. If any of this is resonating with you, then you are in desperate need of cultivating the art of non-action! You simply cannot make any progress spiritually if the way you live your daily life is sapping away your vital forces.

Just as I discussed in the previous section, though, spirituality is never about beating yourself up and thinking of yourself as a bad person. It's about seeing your situation clearly and instituting a practice that begins with small steps and gradually builds momentum over time. Where to start? Perhaps begin with letting go of the impulse to gather more and more material objects. Do you really need that bigger house, that new phone, that flashy car, or that shopping spree? Will it actually make you truly happy? Another great place to start is letting go of the impulse to fill up all your free time with media. Instead of sitting on the phone or watching another TV show, why not take a leisurely walk outdoors with no destination or agenda, sit on the back porch and feel the sun on your face, or do any other contemplative practice that involves resting in stillness?

Speaking of TV shows, have you seen the Netflix series *Tidying Up with Marie Kondo*? It's a popularized presentation of a Japanese Shinto philosophy that is related to what we are talking about here. In each episode, Kondo helps a new client let go of the material possessions that are draining their energy and well-being. She has them pull out every object in their homes and evaluate each one to determine whether it "sparks joy." Those objects that do can stay; everything else is donated, recycled, or thrown away.

If you've already practiced letting go of the big things mentioned earlier, then, when you feel up to it, see if you can Marie Kondo-ize your home. Let go of everything that you do not cherish or do not have a positive relationship with. Then, when you feel up to it, Marie Kondo-ize the rest of your life too. Let go of habits, relationships, jobs, hobbies, foods, identities, and thought patterns that are draining your vital forces. Let go of needing to look a certain way, needing to be seen a certain way, or even needing to be a certain way.

The idea here is not to be an extremist, to push everything and everyone away, or to deny yourself normal comforts. Remember that black-and-white thinking is not conducive to spiritual growth. The whole purpose of this exercise is to find health and wholeness, not to increase conflict and tension. The idea is to gradually, in a sustainable and healthy way, start redirecting your energies away from the material possessions, distractions, and emotional clutter that are sapping your energies. To start to tap into the natural flow of a simple, harmonious life, one that is focused on your real priorities and that makes room for your spiritual growth. To let go of the habit of creating obstacles to the Tao and to instead start living your life like the effortless dance of Carver Ding.

UNEXPECTED AND UNDESIRED OUTCOMES

We have covered four core practices for health and wholeness, but there's some ground left to cover before we finish this chapter. As with any trustworthy tour guide, it is my duty to not only show you the scenic spots along the path but to also point out the areas where the going might get tough or where there may be some hazards to navigate. Although the techniques introduced in this chapter are effective tools for spiritual growth, there are always some potential downsides to any truly transformational spiritual practice. Since this book is about giving you an honest and balanced introduction, let's not avoid talking about some of the potential dark side.

The first danger I want to point out to you is the likelihood that you will experience some impatience on your spiritual journey. Virtually every spiritual explorer, when they first set out, underestimates the time that this journey will take. The human bodymind is not a computer that can be reprogrammed by downloading a software update in a few minutes. The path to healing and wholeness is not a short track that you can sprint through.

In this chapter I have introduced four simple adaptations of the Asian practices of mindfulness, grounding the energy body, universal friendliness, and non-action. None of these are a quick fix. Results will come slowly, almost imperceptibly. They will accumulate over the long term, gradually, and only with continued practice. Authentic change will take months or years; profound transformation will take decades.

Impatience about making progress is detrimental to your spiritual development because it is a source of anxiety and striving, and leads to an artificial goal-oriented attitude. In order to help avoid becoming impatient, my advice would be to start today by writing yourself a letter. In this letter, explain why you are starting out on your spiritual path. What has brought you to this point? What are the places where you feel you are not healed and whole? What are you hoping to get out of starting this journey? Where do you hope you will wind up, and what do you hope you will discover along the way?

Put that letter in an envelope and date it for a full year from today. Now, set it aside and do the practices. Don't worry if you skip a day here or there, or even a week or two once or twice throughout the year. But genuinely try to do them daily, without thinking about any results. Like the *Bhagavad Gita* says, be completely unattached to the fruits of your actions.

At the end of one year of practice, open your letter and reread it. Give a fair assessment of where you are now compared to where you were then. I am sure that, a year from now, you will find that you are still far from perfect, that there still are all kinds of things about yourself that you would like to continue to work on. But I also think it is extremely likely that you will see some positive change has taken place throughout the year. Specifically, I bet you will find that your mind is a little bit calmer and clearer, that you are able to deal with stress a little bit more effectively, that your relationships with others are a little bit softer, and that your daily energies are a little bit more focused on your priorities.

If that's true and you like what you see, then write yourself a new letter and practice for another year. Keep all your letters and compare them from time to time. I think you'll see after five, ten, fifteen years that you are undeniably becoming the new person you envisioned becoming. And that's what an authentic spiritual journey, as opposed to spiritual materialism, is all about: slow, steady, gradual progress toward our goals of healing and wholeness.

Aside from impatience, another common danger on this journey is what many people refer to as a "spiritual ego." This is where your ego co-opts your spiritual practice in order to burnish its own self-image. You'll know that you're suffering from spiritual ego if you start to think of yourself as superior to other people, as if your spiritual practice makes you part of some elite group that is wiser and better than the "ignorant masses." Another sign of spiritual ego is if you start to exhibit a savior complex, acting as if your spiritual practice gives you the power or the responsibility to rescue everyone else from their issues.

Spiritual ego often leads people to be ostentatious and showy in practice. It actually can be quite helpful to have a special space dedicated to your spiritual practice, such as a room or a corner where you do your meditation and grounding techniques. But to make a grand show of your newfound spirituality by filling that space—or your entire house!—with Buddha statues and other spiritual knickknacks is just self-puffery. Another form of ostentation is, say you're out with friends and it's getting late and you want to make sure to get in your thirty-minute practice before bedtime. Do you take leave of your friends discreetly, or do you make a big show of letting everyone know that you are going home to meditate? Using your spirituality for any kind of self-aggrandizement or attention is a sign of a spiritual ego.

Another way spiritual ego frequently manifests is through proselytizing, in which you shift from being an open-minded spiritual explorer to being a salesperson for a particular teaching or viewpoint. Are you convinced that your tradition or system or point of view is the right one for everyone just because it's working for you? Of course, it's natural to want to share with others something wonderful that you have discovered. But ask yourself if that's being done freely and with a light and generous heart. If you have assumed it is your job to convert everyone to your way of thinking, that surely is just your spiritual ego talking.

In the extreme, this kind of spiritual egotism manifests as fundamentalism. Spiritual exploration, as I have defined the term, implies a flexible approach embracing a mixture of different influences and avoiding religious dogmatism. Unfortunately, I have found that it is quite common for people who describe themselves as spiritual to start taking increasingly rigid approaches to their favorite ideas or practices. If you peruse the comments section of popular YouTube videos or Facebook posts related to Asian spiritual traditions, you'll see what I mean. These threads are full of snarky comments, holier-than-thou pontification, bitter disagreements between factions, and other ugliness that is the complete opposite of spiritual exploration. If you find yourself joining in these arguments about whose spiritual system is better, that's just your spiritual ego you're flexing.

Aside from impatience and ego, the last of the dangers I want to talk about here is a rare occurrence among people doing the kinds of practices I have recommended in this chapter. But it is still possible that you might experience a "spiritual emergency." These can take a number of different forms. Some scientists talk about "meditation-related adverse effects," which are unexpected or unwanted psychological effects that are triggered by techniques such as mindfulness and the grounding practices outlined earlier, as well as other practices introduced later in this book. These effects can range from digestive issues and random pains, to heightened symptoms of anxiety or depression, visual or auditory hallucinations, depersonalization/derealization, mania, all the way to full-blown psychosis needing hospitalization.

Spiritual emergencies have recently been receiving more attention both among scholars and spiritual practitioners in the West. I have been actively involved in researching these phenomena among Asian Buddhist practitioners (see, for example, my academic book on this subject called *Meditation Sickness*). The consensus emerging from all of this research is that a small percentage of people may experience anomalous events or unpleasant symptoms as a result of engaging in spiritual practice. These events seem to be much more likely to occur among people who engage in particularly intense periods of practice (such as meditation retreats), those who practice without the guidance of an experienced teacher, and those who have a history of trauma or mental illness. But, unfortunately, it appears that adverse events can happen to even the most experienced practitioners at any time. As with any good medicine, some people occasionally will experience side effects.

Some experiences that are labeled spiritual emergencies are, in my view, actually spiritual openings being misunderstood or misdiagnosed as problems. The practices I have introduced in this chapter are meant to be safe and accessible adaptations of traditional techniques that modern people can use in their daily lives. However, we must remember that the original spiritual practices upon which these are based were never intended primarily as tools for navigating modern life. We are using them that way today, but these contemplative techniques originally were intended to be part of a quest for enlightenment. They were employed primarily by monastics, ascetics, and yogis who were intently focused on rapid and profound personal transformation, and who mainly lived in spiritual communities of like-minded people under the supervision of advanced spiritual teachers.

I discuss various kinds of spiritual experiences in more detail in the next three chapters. But, just to give a few examples, a meditator who suddenly is unable to locate their sense of self may assume that they are experiencing an adverse psychological state called depersonalization. However, it may simply be that they have suddenly opened up to a nondual state of consciousness. Likewise, a meditator suddenly seeing shapes and hearing voices could be having hallucinations, or they could be opening up to spirits or divine guides. A meditator suddenly experiencing electric shock–like sensations in their chest might be having heart palpitations, or they could be experiencing strong energetic fluctuations associated with kundalini.

Spiritual openings or "breakthrough experiences" like these can be dramatic if they happen suddenly. They can be extremely positive, or extremely negative, or just extremely weird. They almost always destabilize your sense of self and the status quo of your life, and they may not be readily recognized by medical or psychiatric professionals who are unfamiliar with spiritual work. If all of that seems like too much of a risk, then I recommend that you take it easy, stick with the core practices I've introduced in this chapter, practice them in moderation, and do not engage in the practices I'll be talking about in chapters 4–6.

To avoid any sudden upheavals, it is always advisable to move slowly and steadily, no matter what practices you are doing. As I said before, think in terms of years not days. If any kind of problems or weird symptoms arise, take a break from practice and have a personal consultation with a spiritual guide or meditation teacher you trust before continuing. If you feel like something comes up that is more than you can handle on your own, reach out to an organization or therapist that is familiar with spiritual emergencies. (There are some handy resources you should know about in box 3.6.)

While spiritual practice is generally safe, it's not like there are zero risks. These practices are not inert; they are psychoactive. Therefore, if at any time the instructions I'm giving in this book seem to be detrimental, or if you encounter something in your practice that feels wrong, no one should judge you for exercising your judgment and walking away. And you shouldn't judge yourself either. Like anything else, these Asian spiritual practices are not for everyone. Whether they are for you, only you can say for sure.

BOX 3.6: Resources for Spiritual Emergencies

Who would wander off for a long trek in the wilderness without knowing a phone number to call in case of emergency? Well, consider this your list of emergency contacts. You probably will never need it, but just in case, you know where to find it.

- American Center for the Integration of Spiritually Transformative Experiences: *https://aciste.org*
- Cheetah House: *https://www.cheetahhouse.org*
- International Spiritual Emergence Network: *https://www.spiritualemergence network.org*
- Spiritual Crisis Network: *https://spiritualcrisisnetwork.uk*
- Spiritual Emergence Anonymous: *https://spiritualemergenceanonymous.org*

The path to healing and wholeness is a long-term, slow, and steady journey. It is about making the time to gently nudge yourself daily in the direction of more mental well-being, energetic groundedness, compassion, and clarity in daily life. I believe that what the vast majority of the readers of this book are looking for will be found in the four simple practices introduced in this chapter. People might be tempted to turn to the later chapters in this book looking for quick fixes, but what I've talked about here is the safest and most effective method of getting most people where they want to go.

If what I have written here feels like it's enough, there is no need for you to read chapters 4–6, which focus on more advanced techniques. Once you have found a camping spot that's perfect for you, just pitch your tent; you are not required to keep wandering deeper into more difficult terrain! On the other hand, those of you who are looking for a journey that is much more adventuresome, definitely challenging, sometimes grueling, possibly even life threatening, please follow me. Watch your step, though. The terrain will be getting rather more difficult from here onward.

CHAPTER 4

EXPLORING NONDUAL PERCEPTION

Wait, did you hear what I just said about the terrain getting difficult? Do not wander lightly into this territory! If you do choose to proceed, be forewarned that, from this point onward, the goals of our exploration will be changing fundamentally. From here, the journey is no longer about seeking well-being and wholeness. In contrast to these forms of self-improvement, Asian spiritual traditions say that in order to become enlightened you need to dismantle the self altogether. The path will get uncomfortable for you because "you" are precisely what these traditions are aiming to get rid of.

One common way of expressing this is to say that Asian spiritual traditions teach ways of transcending our sense of being a "separate self." Another way of saying the same thing is that they teach us to experience reality as nondual. The English word *nonduality* is a translation of the Sanskrit term *advaita*, literally meaning "not-two."

What two things are being unified or realized as never having being separate in the first place? In order to answer this question, it may be useful to start by means of a contrast with Western religions. Generally speaking, mainstream Judaism, Christianity, and Islam have taught that there is a fundamental distinction between God and humanity, between the sacred and the profane, between the holy and the worldly. In most periods of history, and in many places still today, it would be considered blasphemous to claim that you yourself are God. This claim was sometimes even punishable by death. (In fact, that is precisely what got Jesus crucified in the story told in the New Testament!)

Because of this fundamental divide between the divine and the human, mainstream Western religion is primarily concerned with how people can behave according to God's will, how they can have faith in God, perhaps even how they might experience God in some way, but never with how people can become God or realize that they already are God. Asian religions have a completely different emphasis. In direct contradiction to Western traditions, they assert that it is entirely possible—and very desirable—for human beings to merge ourselves with the divine. In many Asian forms of spirituality, in fact, it is said that we all are already divine and just need to become aware of that fact. (I'm using the term *divine* here instead of *God* to emphasize that many Asian traditions don't see "the Ultimate" or "the Absolute" as a personalized, anthropomorphic god but rather as some kind of universal consciousness or everythingness or nothingness.)

How do we merge with the Ultimate or realize our own Absolute nature? All Asian religions agree that the key to doing so is to dismantle our habitual sense that we are a self that is separate from the whole of reality. It is precisely this sense of being divided from the whole that prevents us from seeing our true divine nature. The specific techniques of overcoming this separation vary from tradition to tradition, each often targeting different aspects of the self. At the most basic level, all Asian traditions begin with ethical teachings that encourage people to move past selfishness, self-centeredness, self-aggrandizement, and other kinds of behaviors and habits that continually prop up the feeling of being separate and superior to others. Many traditions then prescribe certain kinds of behaviors and values that further undermine the sense of self: the renunciation of luxury, charity, celibacy, and so forth. Eventually, a number of Asian spiritual traditions turn to teaching contemplative practices that are designed to be powerful tools of self-deconstruction.

EXPERIENCING NONDUALITY

The word *self* refers to an array of diverse psychological and neurological processes. At the most basic level, there's a sense of self associated with perception that is hardwired into your brain. We all experience ourselves as occupying the middle of our sensory field: the visual field is laid out in front of us, and sounds appear in a 360-degree sphere with us at the center. Then there's a bodily sense of self, the sense that I am my body or that it uniquely belongs to me. This is what makes me feel that something happened to "me" when I stub a toe, but not when someone else does.

Another layer of the self is the specific kind of mental activity that is often labeled "the ego." This doesn't necessarily mean being egotistical or narcissistic but refers rather to the locus of identity and action. We see this ego arise in self-referential thoughts like "I'm hungry" or "that person was mean to me" or "I believe in aliens"—that is, whenever we are speaking or thinking of ourselves as an independent entity or agent in the world. We then have sense that this ego has an identity with a name, a birthday, a race, a gender, a personal history, and so forth.

Aside from such internal senses of self, there are also all sorts of social and behavioral selves that emerge when we're with other people. These include habitual roles that we fall into or unconscious ways of interacting with different groups; for example, feeling like a different person when we're at work versus when we're playing with our kids. Sometimes these shifts can be quite unconscious to the individual although other people would instantly notice them. (For example, a friend of mine whose parents are from England but who himself grew up in the US tends to automatically fall into an English accent when he speaks with British people, even though he has no trace of one when he speaks to Americans. When I pointed this out to him, he had no idea it was happening.)

All of these different types of self make up what people generally are referring to when they say "me." And many Asian spiritual traditions are out to dismantle all of these senses of me—perceptual, egoistic, identity based, and social. They do so by analyzing and directly overcoming the sense of self at the most fundamental level: the level of perception.

In order to understand nondual approaches to perception, take a moment to appreciate how your senses are working right now. Take a look at anything around you, or even at the letters in this very sentence. If you are like most people, you would describe yourself as experiencing two things, normally referred to as the object and the subject. That is, you experience not just the letters in this sentence but also a sense that there's a "you" looking at them. The you is "here" and the letters are "over there." If you experience these two facets of perception, we can say that your perception is dualistic.

Nondual practices are designed to collapse that perceptual duality between subject vs. object. (You might also think of it as collapsing the duality of "here" vs. "there" or of "self" vs. "the world.") Asian traditions advocate four main approaches to doing this, which are the focus of the next sections in this chapter.

What is crucial to underscore from the outset is that, while Asian traditions have a lot to say about philosophy, the nondual practices being described in this chapter are not about philosophy or concepts. The effects they are intending to produce are experiential. That is to say, nondual perception is not about thinking in a new way. It's about actually shifting the way you are perceiving reality. The experience of duality collapsing is unmistakable, and experiencing it is completely different than thinking about it. It's like reading about chocolate and thinking about what it might taste like, versus suddenly having a mouthful of it.

How the experience of tasting nonduality comes to pass is different for different people. No one really knows why—Buddhism and Hinduism both will say it's because of past karma—but some people seem to be prone to experiencing the shift more quickly than others. Some might get a taste right at the beginning of their spiritual journey, while others will have to practice intensely for years or decades. Likewise, for some people, when it comes, the experience of nonduality opens up slowly. They gain a little glimpse, then a while later another little glimpse, and slowly these moments build up over time in depth and duration. Other people experience a profound shift all at once. One minute they have no idea what chocolate tastes like and the next they get smacked in the face with a chocolate pie!

At present, there is no way to predict how individual people will experience the shift into nondual perception. Some research with brain stimulation, as well as with psychedelics, is currently underway that may someday make it possible to expose people to the taste of chocolate in a more controlled and predictable way. At the moment, however, this research is still in its infancy, so I won't be discussing it here.

In any event, a shift into nondual perception that takes place slowly over many years or decades tends to feel like a more controlled transition and is often described as a gradual "unfolding" or "deepening." On the other hand, when the shift comes quickly and profoundly, this is often described as a "mystical experience" or an "awakening experience." ("Awakening" can also be used to refer to a slower unfolding when those processes have reached a certain tipping point.) Many people on spiritual journeys crave to have sudden, powerful experiences, but, in fact, the people who have had them often express a feeling of being overwhelmed and wish that things had unfolded more slowly for them.

All of the spiritual practices discussed in the next three chapters are specifically designed to provoke these kinds of radical shifts in your experience of yourself and of reality. Importantly, because the shifts we are talking about are not just shifts in *what* you are perceiving but *how* your perception works—and in later chapters, how your emotions and body work—these changes can often take you by surprise or even be radically destabilizing. Altered states of consciousness may persist for some time (days or weeks or even months) and may require lengthy adjustment periods (weeks or months or even years) before you feel stable enough to function normally again. To mention one particularly notorious example, the popular spiritual teacher Eckhart Tolle says he sat in reverie on a park bench for two years in a state of utter bliss before he could integrate his experience enough to live a somewhat normal life.

All mystical experiences—no matter how intense—are temporary. Sooner or later, the person integrates these and returns to more "normal" functioning. Something to pay attention to, however, is whether the person returns to the same place as before, or if the experience results in a change in their baseline state and a "new normal." Often, the result of a profound nondual experience is that the baseline shifts toward the individual being more selfless, which hopefully also involves being more open, more kind, more aware, more present, and more equanimous. If the baseline is not shifting in this direction over the long term, that's a good indication that the experiences are not actually of a beneficial spiritual nature. This is a good rule of thumb that can help you to distinguish between authentic mystical experiences and hallucinations, mania, psychosis, or just wishful thinking.

However long the process takes, the goal of Asian spiritual traditions is to eventually move the baseline of your normal everyday consciousness further and further into nondual territory. That is to say, the idea is to cultivate enough nondual glimpses or experiences of whatever magnitude to shift you into permanently transcending the self and stabilizing nondual perception. This, in the traditions we're discussing in this chapter, is the one of the primary definitions of an enlightened person.

Ready to get started?

SELF-INQUIRY

The following sections are intended to give you a brief orientation to four different approaches to cultivating nondual perception. Once you are oriented to the general outlines and some of the basic vocabulary I provide here, you will know what you are looking for when you seek out more detailed information elsewhere. I have also provided some resources for you at the end of the chapter.

One of the most common ways of overcoming the subject/object duality of ordinary perception is to collapse the object into the subject. Techniques aiming in this direction are primarily found

in Hindu forms of practice, although there are also Buddhist variations such as the Chinese *kanhua* technique. Perhaps the technique
that is most well known in the West comes from Advaita Vedanta
and its modern form, neo-Advaita, usually just called "Advaita" by
practitioners.

The principal method in contemporary Advaita is called "self-
inquiry practice." In this particular approach to nonduality, rather
than focusing on what is perceived (the objects), we are focusing
on the perceiver (the subject). This technique was popularized
among Western spiritual seekers by the most prominent sages
of the neo-Advaita movement, Ramana Maharshi (usually simply
called "Ramana") and H. W. L. Poonja (commonly called "Papaji"
by his followers).

A practice inspired by Ramana is outlined in box 4.1. The technique is simple. It involves the persistent contemplation of the
question "Who am I?" or "What am I?" This question isn't asking

BOX 4.1: Getting Started with Self-Inquiry Practice

Self-inquiry is a contemplation or reflection that you can do at any point during
the day, but you should also set aside some dedicated time to practice. Review
some of the considerations that we talked about in the section on mindfulness in
chapter 3, particularly regarding timing and setting.

Relax your body and try to minimize distractions. After a few minutes, when
you feel fairly relaxed and focused, drop the question "Who am I?" or "What am
I?" into your mindstream.

Don't go to your thoughts to formulate an intellectual answer to the question.
The idea is not to try to answer the question at all but to just relax and see what
happens in response to asking it.

Give it a bit of time—a couple of minutes perhaps—and then drop the question into your relaxed mind again. Repeat over and over again for the duration of
the practice session.

Don't worry that nothing is happening. For a long time, it will seem like it's
not working. But, eventually, you will feel something shift.

(continues)

One last piece of advice involves what to do if you think you have arrived at an answer for your question. If you think you found the answer to your inquiry question, and that answer is anything other than experiencing yourself as the all-pervasive cosmic awareness, then ask yourself "What is witnessing *that*?"

For example, if your answer to "What am I?" is that you are a soul, then what is witnessing that soul? If your answer is that you are an inner spirit, then what is witnessing that inner spirit? If your answer is the thought that you are God, then what is witnessing that thought? Keep going until you've exhausted your mind and you experience a profound shift in identity.

Enjoy, and remember that the exercises introduced in this book are only intended to dip your toe into a deeply complex system of practice. If you connect with this practice and think it might be useful for you, it is best to explore this territory with a knowledgeable teacher who can give you personalized guidance. In addition, you can consult the additional resources at the end of this chapter.

you to describe the attributes of the self but to move beyond them. Your mission is to discover who is actually looking out of your eyes. Who is actually the witness of all phenomena? That witness can't be "Pierce," because everything that I could possibly call "Pierce"—this body, these thoughts, these emotions, these memories, etc.—are themselves objects appearing inside my consciousness, not the one actually doing the looking. Anything that I could call "Pierce" is simply phenomena or perceptions arising in my awareness, not the one who is aware.

Phenomenology

Continuing this line of inquiry persistently, ideally one will experience a diminishing of the usual sense of self, which eventually leads to a shift in identity. A shift in identity means that I no longer see myself as Pierce, a father, a professor, an author, a man, or even a human being. I am no longer my body, mind, emotions, memories, or any combination of the above. Those are all objects, not the subject. By ruling out all phenomena as not being who or what I am, I am left with only the bare sense of being conscious, the bare sense of being aware. This is simply the feeling of "I exist" or "I am." I am the awake, aware subject that witnesses all objects.

Again, I am not describing a philosophy for you to think about here, or an ontological truth claim about how reality is, but rather a phenomenological experience that can be had through this particular kind of contemplative practice. The difference between thinking about chocolate and actually experiencing chocolate is unmistakable. The experience of realizing that you are awareness is distinctive, like the whole cosmos has been flipped inside-out. One moment you feel like you are a person in the world, and the next you feel like you are just consciousness with the world, including the person you thought you were, now arising inside of You!

From this vantage point, all phenomena seem to be made out of consciousness. In the traditional way of saying it, I realize that *atman* is *Brahman*. In other words, who I am is none other than the singular consciousness that makes up all reality.

In English, Brahman or the cosmic consciousness is often referred to as the Self, with a capital S, in contrast to the small individual self. As people sink into this shift of identity from self to Self, they often feel that they are a clear, awake presence. As the implications of this shift become clear, an immense joy may arise for no reason in particular. An unshakeable sense that everything would be OK no matter what happens. Some ways of speaking that previously seemed like gibberish now make perfect sense. The only aspect of time that exists is an eternal present moment, because the whole notion of "the past" or "the future" is simply an idea that's arising right this moment in the awareness that is me. The only aspect of space that exists is an omnipresent "here," because the whole notion of there being anywhere else other than here is simply an idea that's arising right here in the awareness that is me. The only thing in the entire cosmos that can possibly exist is this Brahman, this great Self, this one vast witness that I am, because the whole notion of there being anything other than me is simply an idea that's arising within me. There can be no such thing as reality outside of awareness. Awareness is all that exists—or could ever exist. Everything is awareness.

Again, this is not a thought experiment but an actual experiential change in identity. In the language of the *Chandogya Upanishad*, quoted in chapter 2, I look around at the world and, no matter what I am looking at, I truly see that "I Am That." I am everything in the universe. I am the Cosmos itself. I am the One. I am Brahman. I am God.

INSIGHT MEDITATION

The second approach to nonduality is the direct inverse of the first in that now we will be collapsing the subject into the object. Another way of saying the same thing is that we will see that the subject is not actually a subject after all, but just another object. When the subject side of the subject/object duality is emptied out, it leaves us only with objects. There is no witness, no consciousness, no awareness, just phenomena.

This is the primary approach to nonduality embraced by nearly all forms of Buddhism. In fact, the emptying out of the subject is the signature move of Buddhism, what distinguishes it from most other Indian spiritual systems. As with the previous section, my intention here is to provide just the briefest of overviews, since there are many other resources related to the practice of Buddhism that are easily accessible elsewhere.

The Buddha declared as one of his fundamental teachings that all phenomena have three characteristics: impermanence, suffering, and non-self. That is to say, all objects of perception are bound to change eventually, all are bound to produce suffering if we cling to them, and no phenomenon constitutes anything like a self. The term used for this lack of self, *anatman*, is specifically negating the Sanskrit term *atman*, that is, not just the existence of an independent individual soul but also anything else that might be pointed to as an unchanging being, true inner essence, divine entity, or Self.

As said in the passages from *The Discourse on Evidence of Self-lessness* I quoted in box 2.2, the Buddha taught that what people think of as a self is merely a collection of discrete parts or functions, called "heaps" (*skandhas*). These included the physical body, feelings, perceptions, mental fabrications (including thoughts and memories), and consciousness. But none of these add up to a self. As we saw in the discourse, the Buddha taught that all of these are to be understood as "This is not mine, I am not this, this is not my self."

This focus on negation is the opposite of the kind of affirmation we saw in the *Chandogya Upanishad*, also quoted in chapter 2, where the young Svetaketu learns to look at the world and see everything as identical with who he is. Whereas the follower of Advaita experiences all-pervasive awareness or consciousness as the foundational essence of the cosmos, the Buddha insists that consciousness too is just another heap to be negated as impermanent, a cause of suffering, and not a self.

There are many Buddhist methods that were developed to provoke a direct experience of non-self. One of the most popularly available in the West is the technique called "insight meditation," or in the Pali language, vipassana. A beginning vipassana practice is described in box 4.2, on the next page. As you will see, the practice involves spending time closely examining the flow of one's perceptual experience, tracking each sight, sound, feeling, thought, and so forth, that arises. As each of these experiences arise, you meet them with the knowledge that they are impermanent, liable to cause suffering, and devoid of any self-like essence.

For it to work, this practice needs to be applied with relentless rigor. Those three characteristics must be applied equally to any and all experiences that arise, no matter what. Your cherished memories from the past? Impermanent, suffering, non-self. The love you feel for your child or your pet? Impermanent, suffering, non-self. The stabbing feeling of pain in your knee that is really making you want to uncross your legs? You get the picture.

BOX 4.2: Getting Started with Vipassana Practice

Start by reviewing the considerations that we talked about in the section on mindfulness in chapter 3 regarding timing and setting. Take a seat in a comfortable chair or on a meditation cushion where you can remain upright but relaxed. You might choose to do some mindfulness of breathing meditation for a few minutes to get focused. When you feel ready, shift into vipassana mode.

For vipassana, you may continue to focus on your breath if you want, or pay attention to your body sensations, or hearing, or thinking, or any other kind of sensory experience. Different teachers focus on different objects, but which object you choose is far less important than how you approach it.

For this example, let's say that you've chosen to cycle between vision, hearing, and body sensations. Start by placing your attention on your visual field. Although your eyes are closed, you are still able to perceive little specks of light flitting about. Closely monitor those, observing their color, movement, and interplay. Notice how none of these flecks of light are permanent, how clinging to them in any way would cause you unnecessary suffering, and how none of them represent a self or a permanent essence.

After several minutes, transition to observing the sounds you hear. Closely monitor these, observing their timbre and tone, but not using your mind to try to identify the source of the sound. It doesn't matter what sounds you hear, or how many, or how loud, or whatever. Just open up your sense of hearing to the symphony of sounds all around you. Notice how none of these sounds are permanent, how clinging to them in any way would cause you unnecessary suffering, and how none of them represent a self or a permanent essence.

Next, turn to observing your body sensations. You might sweep your attention over your body from head to toe and back again, or rest your attention in the center of your abdomen and feel the whole body from there. Either way, closely monitor the sensations you feel. Again, it doesn't matter what the sensations are—heat, cold, an itch, pressure, prickling, or more subtle feelings that don't have names—treat them all the same. Notice how none of these sensations are permanent, how clinging to them in any way would cause you unnecessary suffering, and how none of them represent a self or a permanent essence.

Crucially, as you do this meditation, you will inevitably notice that your attention has wandered off of your chosen object—most likely it will do so many times. Frequently, it will wander over to another one of the three objects, which is perfectly fine. It may also wander to your other senses of smell or taste, which is also no problem. Just pick up the meditation from there and continue noticing that the new sensory stimuli are impermanent, causes of suffering, and devoid of self.

Additionally, there will be many times during your practice that your attention wanders to mental objects. These may be thoughts in the form of words, thoughts in the form of visual stimuli, memories, emotions, or other kinds of mental activity. When this happens, treat these mental phenomena just like you did the other phenomena. Buddhism considers the mind to be another "sense gate" or "sense door," just like vision, hearing, touch, and the rest. So, the same technique applies just as with all the other senses. Notice how none of these thoughts are permanent, how clinging to them in any way would cause you unnecessary suffering, and how none of them represent a self or a permanent essence. Apply this especially to the thoughts you feel are correct, urgent, or existentially meaningful.

You might spend several minutes on each of the sense doors or allow your attention to float freely between all of them. Whatever best allows you to maintain your focus is the right choice for you.

Enjoy, and remember that the exercises introduced in this book are only intended to dip your toe into a deeply complex system of practice. If you connect with this practice and think it might be useful for you, it is best to explore this territory with a knowledgeable teacher who can give you personalized guidance. In addition, consult the additional resources at the end of this chapter.

Phenomenology

By repeatedly reinforcing non-self in this way on a moment-by-moment basis, eventually, there may be either a breakthrough experience or a more gradual process in which the sense of being a self drops away. Here, it's less of a shift in identity, as was the case in the previous section, than a disappearance of identification altogether. As with before, I am no longer Pierce, a father, a professor, an author, a man, or a human being. I am no longer my body, mind, emotions, memories, or any combination of the above. But I do not identify as consciousness or awareness or anything else either. The need to identify disappears altogether. All of the phenomena and perceptions are still arising as they always were, but they seem not to be arising "in" anything or "for" anyone. Any self-referential thought or any feeling that I am a self that might arise for me is seen as just one more phenomenon to be negated, not a true reflection of reality.

Again, experiencing this is completely different from thinking about it, and the moment it flips is uncanny and unmistakable. One moment you are there watching the world go by, and the next the world is still going by but "you" are completely absent. Instead of your usual sense of being a separate self, you feel a palpable sense of absence, emptiness, void. Sinking more deeply into this realization over time leads to tranquility, equanimity, and a sense that everything is perfect just as it is. There's nothing to do and nowhere to go. And how could there be, when there's no one there to do anything or go anywhere? Things just happen of their own accord. Life flows freely. What needs to be taken care of somehow gets done, but no one is managing or controlling any of it.

Eventually, the recognition of non-self extends not only to your sense of self but equally to all other phenomena. Not only is no individual perception or thought or sensation "you," but you also see that nothing else exists as a separate object either. Everything you perceive seems hollow and unsubstantial, lacking in solidity or essence, in a way similar to a mirage or to dream images. There is a spacious quality to all phenomena as they arise, as if they were mere bubbles or the shimmery translucence of a rainbow. In the language used by Buddhism, everything is seen as being "empty." Following this progression further may lead to a "cessation" event, which I will discuss in the next section.

MEDITATIVE ABSORPTION

The next approach does not use analysis or investigation in the way the previous two exercises did. Instead, the idea is to use meditation to cultivate a deep stillness of the mind. Doing so in a methodical way can help one to sequentially unlock subtler and subtler states of consciousness, which culminate in nondual realization.

This approach is most commonly associated with the Theravada school of Buddhism, as well as with certain forms of Hindu practice, such as Transcendental Meditation and Patañjali's *Yoga Sutras* among others. Each of these systems prescribes their own techniques regarding how to develop stillness, as well as their own ideas about the various levels, stages, or benchmarks of concentration that one achieves as one makes progress. There is way too much detail to be able to adequately describe or compare them here. As with previous sections, my purpose is merely to summarize these practices in very general terms to give you an indication of how they fit into the overall picture of Asian spirituality and to point you in a direction that might be interesting for you to travel.

Hindu forms of meditative absorption, not surprisingly, aim at the Hindu version of nonduality. The goal is to immerse oneself fully in the sense that "I Am," or in pure consciousness, or in unity with Brahman. Hindu systems recognize a number of stages of meditative absorption, which they call *samadhis*. The exact number and description of these stages vary. The Transcendental Meditation system developed by Maharishi Mahesh Yogi, for example, recognizes seven states of consciousness in total. The first three are the ordinary states of waking, dreaming, and dreamless sleep that we all experience. Then, through dedicated long-term meditation practice, a practitioner can develop higher states that are called Transcendental, Cosmic, God, and Unity consciousness.

The trajectory laid out in Patañjali's *Yoga Sutras* also involves seven stages, but they are different than the Transcendental Meditation ones. The general trajectory is that one begins to develop concentration on a meditation object to the point that the thinking mind falls away leaving bliss. Further concentration leads to bliss falling away and leaving just the sense of "I Am." From there, the meditator continues to deepen, eventually reaching a state of absorption beyond all conceptualization (*nirvikalpa-samadhi*). Here, all that is left is pure consciousness with no objects of even the most subtle kind.

The Theravada Buddhist model of concentration practice is similar to these Hindu models in some ways, with the major difference that instead of pure consciousness it aims toward the cessation of consciousness altogether (called *nibbana* or *nirvana*). This system enumerates eight stages of meditative absorptions, which it calls *jhanas*. Again, as the meditator begins to develop concentration on the meditation object, they transcend the thinking mind and then also bliss. They then begin to enter the upper *jhanas*, experiences of infinite space, infinite consciousness, infinite void, and a state beyond perception and non-perception. This trajectory culminates in what is called "cessation" (*nirodha-samāpatti*), often considered the ninth and highest *jhana*, where consciousness itself blacks out and any form of experience stops altogether.

What are the specific meditation techniques that are used to develop meditative absorption? Some traditional meditation objects used for this purpose include mantras, a candle flame, and colored disks called *kasinas*. The mindfulness of breath meditation, which I described in chapter 3, can also be modified to focus on developing concentration. In box 4.3, I describe a mantra meditation that uses the Sanskrit word *OM*. This mantra, said to be the sound of the cosmos, is commonly used when beginning concentration practice in many types of Hindu practice, but there are other mantras that are commonly used in different traditions. Various schools of Buddhism use mantras such as BUDDHO in Theravada, OM MANI PADME HUM in Tibetan, NAMO AMITUOFO in Chinese, and NAM MYOHO RENGE KYO in Japanese. In Hinduism, there are a great number of different mantras associated with different deities. In Transcendental Meditation, you are given your own personalized mantra that is said to be specifically optimized for you.

BOX 4.3: Getting Started with Mantra Practice

Start by reviewing the considerations that we talked about in the section on mindfulness in chapter 3 regarding timing and setting. Take a seat in a comfortable chair or on a meditation cushion where you can remain upright but relaxed. Close your eyes and take a few breaths to relax your body.

When you are ready, let yourself breathe normally and drop the word *OM* into your mindstream. Say it either mentally or out loud, and say it slowly, letting it resonate a bit. Pay close attention to the reverberations of the word. When you feel that the word has faded away or that your mind is becoming distracted by other stimuli, say the word again.

Repeat OM over and over again every few minutes for the entire duration of the practice. The idea is for the word to occupy all of your mindspace. Any time you feel drawn to something else, repeat the mantra. However, beware of gripping too tightly to any object of meditation. Concentration doesn't mean forcing the mind to focus; it's more like inviting the mantra to take up as much of your awareness as possible.

When starting out, some people find it beneficial to use a set of mala beads to help keep track of the recitations. Typically, a mala has 108 beads, culminating in a knot. Hold the mala in your hand, pressing the first bead after the knot with your fingers. Now, each time you say your mantra during meditation, move your fingers to the next bead. You'll know that you've gone around the full circle when you are back at the knot again. It may be the case that adding this physical movement into your practice helps your mind to stabilize on the mantra, but if the mala becomes distracting to your practice, then simply set it down.

At some point, you will likely find that the mantra begins coming to mind even when you are not formally meditating. This is considered a good thing. Whenever you have a quiet moment or a break in the action during your normal day, instead of pulling out your phone or doing some other mindless activity, think about the mantra. In this way, let it become a constant companion throughout your life.

It will help you to progress if you also minimize distractions that scatter your concentration in your daily life. Avoid spending a lot of time doing activities that encourage your attention to wander quickly from one object to another. For example, scrolling through a social media feed is the opposite kind of mental experience than we are cultivating here and may detract from your training.

You should be aware that, initially, most people experience a lot of resistance when they start cultivating concentration. It can feel boring, like a chore, or even like excruciating torture! However, little by little, over the long term, you should experience your mind gradually becoming more focused and still.

Eventually, you will be able to sit in meditation and be absorbed in your mantra for the whole session without feeling any resistance. At some point, it will even start to feel pleasant and you will look forward to your meditation time. (In Buddhism, this is sometimes called "access concentration," *upacara-samadhi*.) You are now ready to start exploring higher states of consciousness using meditative absorption.

(continues)

Enjoy, and remember that the exercises introduced in this book are only in-tended to dip your toe into a deeply complex system of practice. If you connect with this practice and think it might be useful for you, it is best to explore this territory with a knowledgeable teacher who can give you personalized guidance. In addition, consult the additional resources at the end of this chapter.

Phenomenology

Traversing the path of meditative absorption is not for the faint of heart. It usually requires a ton of time and effort because these levels of concentration and stillness are not easy to develop. How-ever, in the long run, these systems cause deep and comprehensive transformations in how practitioners perceive reality. Long-term meditators in these traditions are able to see clearly how perception works with a granularity that is unavailable to people who have not developed such heightened powers of concentration.

A modern metaphor that is commonly used to talk about this is the frame-rate of a movie. Most people are watching life go by as one continuous stream of phenomena and activity, as if they are watching a movie on a screen. However, meditators who have developed high levels of concentration can perceive that the film is actually made up of an endless stream of still photos. It's only because these images are being shown in succession at such a rapid frame rate that there appears to be any continuity. Meditators can see that our consciousness is similarly pulsing in a series of brief flashes that last fractions of a second.

Meditators who can watch consciousness happening at this high level of resolution understand how the mind is working from moment to moment, how phenomena arise and pass away, and how the fabric of reality is seemingly created through perception. Ultimately, they see through or beyond even the rapid-fire manifes-tations of phenomena. It's like you stop focusing on the still images that make up the movie altogether and see the black background between the frames, the void beyond or behind or between the ever-changing moments of consciousness.

However momentary, such an experience (or, rather, lack of experience in the Buddhist case) is said to completely and permanently transform the individual. In both Hindu and Buddhist systems, these attainments are said to overcome anger, lust, greed, selfishness, and all other undesirable states. Someone who has seen this level of reality can no longer identify with the small sense of self and thus is liberated from everything that identification with it entails.

DOING NOTHING

The fourth major way that Asian traditions collapse that perceptual duality between subject and object is often called the "pathless path." This approach says that your perception already is nondual, and there is actually nothing you need to train yourself to do. You already are perceiving reality just like an enlightened person; you just don't realize it.

This kind of approach is found in early Taoist writings, in certain varieties of Zen, in the Tibetan schools of Dzogchen and Mahamudra, and in a type of neo-Advaita that is usually referred to as "radical nonduality." The latter is the most extreme form. In radical nonduality, teachers often say that there is absolutely nothing that can be done in terms of spiritual practice. Any attempt to change the way you perceive reality through any type of formal practice is a misguided effort that only serves to reinforce the notion of being a self that can exert control over life. You must simply stop seeking anything, full stop.

The other pathless-path approaches suggest more concrete steps than this. In most cases, there is a preliminary practice of some kind to prepare you for nondual realization. In some forms of Zen, for example, it is common to start off with a simple concentration meditation such as counting your breaths. In other forms of Zen, you are given a *koan*, which is like a nonsensical inquiry that is designed to lead you beyond conceptual thinking. In Tibetan Buddhism, there are usually detailed preliminary practices called *ngöndro*, which can involve receiving blessings or empowerments from a guru, doing thousands of mantra recitations, and other kinds of ritual preparations before you receive the "pointing out instructions" that begin your journey into nonduality.

In the doing-nothing approach, after whatever required preliminary practices are complete, the practitioner spends their time engaged in a kind of meditation that is completely unstructured and effortless. Unlike in all the other forms of practice listed in this book, where there is something you are supposed to "do,"

BOX 4.4: Getting Started with Doing-Nothing Meditation

Start by reviewing the considerations that we talked about in the section on mindfulness in chapter 3 regarding timing and setting. Take a seat in a comfortable chair or on a meditation cushion where you can remain upright but relaxed. Close your eyes and take a few breaths to relax your body.

Now do nothing.

Actually, it's best not to try to do nothing, because that's doing something. Instead, just relax whenever you feel you might be doing something.

Don't be on constant alert, like a dog waiting for the mailman. Just relax. And each time you catch your mind trying to control, manipulate, filter, monitor, or comment on experience, just relax that too. Each time you catch yourself feeling like you need to focus better, or stay alert, or stop thinking, or tend to any other agenda whatsoever, just relax that impulse. And when you get the impulse that you need to relax more, you guessed it, relax that too!

Instead of doing anything, just be. That's it.

Enjoy, and remember that the exercises introduced in this book are only intended to dip your toe into a deeply complex system of practice. If you connect with this practice and think it might be useful for you, it is best to explore this territory with a knowledgeable teacher who can give you personalized guidance. In addition, consult the additional resources at the end of this chapter.

here the goal is to just "rest in the natural state" or to "just sit." You don't control your attention to focus on specific perceptions or inquiries. Instead, you simply accept whatever is happening in your consciousness. If you find yourself trying to control your experience, you simply let go of that effort.

Believe it or not, it's actually really hard to do nothing. When you first start out, you'll probably find that your mind is constantly running around trying to do something. You'll try to stop it, but then you'll realize that trying to stop doing something is also a form of doing something. Your mind may get itself tied up in knots trying to figure out the paradox of how it could possibly start doing nothing. But eventually, your system will find a way to just let go of the conundrum and relax into non-reactivity. Only then can true doing-nothing meditation even begin. Now, you just allow everything that comes along to just be, resting in a state of non-doing and non-striving.

Phenomenology

The power of this practice to overcome duality lies in the insight that the subject/object duality is in the first place actually generated by thought. Once you are able to relax the mind's propensity to constantly control, manipulate, filter, monitor, and comment on experience, you will find that the mind is actually naturally already nondual. In its natural state (in Tibetan called *rigpa*), the mind is clear or pristine. Resting in this state of clarity and non-action, the dualities now effortlessly unwind themselves. You see that the sense of being a separate self or observer was all along just a side effect of your constantly thinking that that was the case.

What you are left with when the mind is doing nothing is impossible to express in words. Because words and concepts are part of the mental activity that you have dropped, they cannot possibly capture the essence of your experience. This impossibility is what is meant in the first two lines of the first chapter of the principal

Taoist scripture, the *Tao Te Ching*, quoted in box 2.4: "The Tao that can be spoken is not the eternal Tao. The name that can be named is not the eternal name." The Tao is the nonduality that lies beyond the concepts and representations of our thinking mind. So, if you can speak about it or name it, then it can't be the Tao.

Practitioners of the doing-nothing approach realize that the Tao isn't "out there" somewhere, located in some hard-to-reach mystical state. It's right here, in the way you see a flower or taste a cup of coffee or feel the shower water against your skin—in all of the ordinary experiences of life prior to us thinking about them. Reality unfolds naturally and effortlessly, without needing any added mental overlay. When all the mental meddling of "doing" ceases, your experience becomes completely uncontrived and spontaneous. Some Buddhist traditions try to capture this by saying that all phenomena are "self-liberated": reality arises just so, perfectly ordinary and perfectly free to be whatever it is. There's no reason to practice to become enlightened: the whole universe is already fully enlightened, just the way it already is.

DETOURS ON THE PATH

The approaches to nonduality outlined here can lead to wondrous and profoundly positive transformations. However, as with all spiritual practices, there can also sometimes be unpredictable or undesirable outcomes.

Let's discuss some potential unpredictable outcomes first. I mentioned in the previous chapter that you need to be aware that these practices are psychoactive and may provoke a sudden and intense mystical or awakening experience. This only happens to a minority of people, as most will experience a more gradual process of unfolding. However, you might be one of those people whose bodyminds are configured to have more dramatic shifts. If so, just being aware that this is a possibility can be helpful in gaining your footing, as even an extremely positive mystical experience can be profoundly discombobulating.

Another unpredictability you should be aware of is that the process of nondual realization is not nearly as straightforward or linear as might be suggested by my brief introductory sections. For example, I have a friend who was practicing a kind of Buddhist insight meditation that was designed to see through the sense of "I" and lead to a realization of non-self. However, as her practice progressed, instead of disappearing altogether, her sense of self began to destabilize and behave unpredictably. She described to me how, after one meditation session, her sense of self detached from her own body and affixed to a tree she was looking at. She then had the bizarre experience of feeling as if she were the tree looking back at a human body that was not her. Fortunately, this experience didn't persist very long at all, but it certainly was weird while it lasted. Keep in mind that there is no way that any book or teacher can list out every possible glitch that might take place when you are engaging in these kinds of practices. Again, just being aware that these types of things can happen, and that they are temporary, can be helpful.

Another possibility to be aware of is that the practice of one nondual approach may lead to an experience that normally is expected to come from a different approach. It's entirely possible, for example, to be practicing a style of doing-nothing meditation and to experience "I Am That." Or to be doing self-inquiry and to experience non-self. It is also very possible that doing one of the practices in this chapter will lead to results that are spoken about in other chapters, such as a heart opening, perceiving entities, kundalini, or other energetic phenomena. If you are locked into a particular spiritual tradition, your teachers may respond to a situation like this by telling you that you've done something wrong, by telling you to ignore what is happening, or by telling you that you've had an "inferior" insight that is actually a delusion. In my experience, it's probably just a sign that you have a particular propensity toward a different approach and that you might want to consider changing up your practice to suit your natural affinities.

I'd also like to remind you here of the warnings about spiritual emergency in the final section of the previous chapter. It is critical to be aware when you are engaging in any of these practices that they are designed to dismantle your sense of self. This is emphatically not about stress reduction or better productivity at work. As the deconstruction process gets underway, you may experience bliss, peace, and tranquility. But as it proceeds you are almost guaranteed to also experience at some point intense discomfort, distress, terror, and other strong reactions. Be absolutely certain that that is what you actually want to do before you start down this path, and seek help from knowledgeable guides, therapists, and teachers who know this territory as you go. (If you don't experience such things eventually, this is quite likely a sign that you are not actually doing the deconstruction work.)

Another undesirable outcome you should be aware of is falling into a mental trap. You might, for example, get trapped in a cycle of endless seeking. Many people hear about nondual awakening and desperately want to experience it. They either devote themselves to a single practice that they pour all of their time into, or they set out to try all kinds of techniques and teachings seeking the one that's going to work for them. Either one of these things is fine to do for a little while when you first start out, but sometimes the quest can go on for decades or even a whole lifetime without leading to any fruition. Such people often become addicted to the spiritual pursuit itself. The seeking itself has become the goal.

A similar danger is getting trapped in a conceptual understanding of nonduality. It frequently happens that people mistake an intellectual understanding of nonduality with nondual realization itself. I have tried to make clear in this chapter that there is a huge gulf between understanding nonduality as a concept and experiencing it directly firsthand. I've mentioned several times that the latter is unmistakable: it's a clear, obvious, and shocking shift in how you experience yourself and how you perceive reality. If you think you know what nonduality is but have not experienced a visceral transformation in your consciousness or perception, you almost certainly have a merely conceptual understanding. Fooling yourself into thinking that you've already arrived can potentially become a lifelong detour that prevents you from ever actually experiencing nonduality.

Yet another trap is to have actually had a certain amount of realization but become addicted to the highs of mystical or awakening experiences. The feeling of an awakening experience is a powerful draw, and once you come back to your baseline, it is normal to feel a certain level of craving to recreate the experience. This, however, is a completely wrongheaded approach. Don't become a spiritual experience junkie, always jonesing for your next fix and trying to game the system in order to make it happen. The important thing to pay attention to is not the highs of the peak experiences but the shifting baseline. How are these experiences changing your perspective on daily life? The way you are with loved ones? Your general level of gentleness, kindness, and equanimity?

If you think you might be trapped in endless seeking, locked in a conceptual understanding, or are turning into an experience junkie, then I think it might be best to only practice "doing nothing" for a while. Spend some time letting go of all your expectations, conceptualizations, and grasping. If this doesn't work to alleviate the symptoms, you could also consider leaving behind spiritual practices that focus on perception altogether. The next two chapters turn to the heart and the body, both of which can be excellent counterbalances to the pitfalls of the approaches presented here.

Turning to the heart and the body is also a great antidote to the last undesirable outcome I'll mention: spiritual bypassing. I'll talk more about spiritual bypassing in chapter 7. For the moment, let's define bypassing as the mistaken notion that nondual perception is going to fix everything that's wrong with your life once you experience it. Or, if you have some access to nondual perception already, another form of spiritual bypassing is using those states to avoid dealing with the messiness of the "real world" or even to deny its existence altogether. Both the Hindu realization of being pure consciousness or the Buddhist realization of non-self can create a feeling of aloofness or detachment from life and from other beings. If you find yourself in that situation, keep reading!

————————

The methods discussed in this chapter are enormously complex systems of practice with thousands of years of history and dozens or hundreds of variations. This chapter has provided a basic outline of some practices and their intended phenomenological results. However, this is only a preliminary scaffolding that needs to be built upon. My intention is for you to use the descriptions and introductory exercises in this chapter to cut through the glut of information and figure out what direction is the most resonant for you. Once you've oriented yourself to where you want to go, then it's up to you to seek out additional information that will help you take concrete steps toward your chosen goal. The resources on the next page are meant to help you to get more information about teachers and techniques related to the practices introduced here.

Please note that there are many Asian spiritual practices that are not mentioned in this book, and there are many approaches to nonduality that are not covered in this chapter. Sometimes, it is because these practices are relatively obscure in the West. Sometimes, it is because they require initiation into a particular religious group before you are allowed to receive the teachings, which goes against the exploratory spirit of this book. In these pages, I am only presenting examples of practices that are openly available to Western spiritual explorers who are curious but not ready to convert to a particular religious tradition. The books and other media I recommend often contain additional information about other practices not mentioned here.

BOX 4.5: Additional Resources
for Exploring Nondual Perception

PODCASTS

- *Buddha at the Gas Pump*—Interviews with spiritual teachers of all kinds. Keyword-search the past episodes to find teachers affiliated with different approaches mentioned in this chapter, and then listen to the interviews to sample their teachings.
- *Awareness Explorers*—Introduction to awareness-based nondual exercises with guided meditations and occasional teacher interviews.

BOOKS

- Greg Goode, *The Direct Path: A User Guide*—Get started with inquiry practice
- Joseph Goldstein, *Insight Meditation: The Practice of Freedom*—Get started with insight meditation
- Stephen Snyder and Tina Rasmussen, *Practicing the Jhanas: Traditional Concentration Meditation as Presented by the Venerable Pa Auk Sayadaw*—Get started with Buddhist concentration practice
- Rebecca Li, *Illumination: A Guide to the Buddhist Method of No-Method*—Get started with doing-nothing meditation

CHAPTER 5

EXPLORING THE HEART

The previous chapter introduced the core practices from multiple traditions of Asian spirituality that lead to the attainment of nondual perception. While they each differ in their ontological truth claims and in their phenomenology, all of these techniques share a common ground: they are targeting your perceptual system. By practicing these methods, you can experience a shift in how you see, hear, feel, and otherwise perceive reality. In contrast, this chapter focuses not on changing how you are perceiving reality but on your relationship to the reality you are experiencing.

Here I will be presenting a number of practices that are intended to open the heart. These practices can be done either in tandem with techniques focusing on shifting your perception or on their own. If you have not had the shifts of identity described in the previous chapter, then open-heartedness will feel like you are more connected with and more receptive to other beings. Alternatively, if you have gone through the kinds of shifts discussed in the previous chapter, then you may not have a sense of a "me" and "others" to be in relationship. Still, open-heartedness can affect the quality of the sensations that arise, producing a feeling of greater intimacy, a heightened sense of presence, and more warmth to your overall experience.

Open-heartedness is a highly valued part of the spiritual path in many Hindu and Buddhist approaches. The path of the heart can lead to enormous fulfillment and high levels of realization, and represents a perfectly valid approach in and of itself. In fact, many people naturally feel more drawn to paths of the heart than to the techniques described in the previous chapter. Do you remember the story I told in chapter 1 about how my spiritual path really opened up for me when I abandoned vipassana meditation and took up metta? Well, that shift was followed by a period of almost twenty years when the path of the heart was the only kind of spiritual activity I was involved in. The moral of that story is to do what works for you. Don't listen to anyone who insists that there's only one way of navigating the spiritual territory.

CULTIVATING COMPASSION

Compassion is a core virtue in nearly all of the world's religions, and no one has a monopoly on it. However, several Asian spiritual traditions teach methods of actively cultivating compassion through specific techniques.

For example, compassionate service to others is a central part of Hinduism. In Sanskrit, one whose spiritual path is primarily dedicated to serving others (in Sanskrit called *seva*) is said to be a practitioner of Karma Yoga, or "the yoga of action." The practitioner of Karma Yoga practices good deeds for the benefit of others. They do so with equanimity, not attached to the outcomes and not interested in self-aggrandizement or personal gain. The foundational Hindu scripture, the *Bhagavad Gita*, mentions Karma Yoga along with Bhakti Yoga (the yoga of devotion, discussed later in this chapter) and Jñana Yoga (the yoga of knowledge, referring to self-inquiry and philosophical approaches discussed in chapter 4). These three spiritual disciplines represent three different and equally effective paths leading to *moksha* or liberation.

Buddhism also places compassion in high regard. In early Buddhism and in the contemporary Theravada tradition, compassion is considered one of the chief attributes of a Buddha and one of the virtues that should be cultivated by anyone who wishes to follow his teachings. In Mahayana Buddhism, compassion is elevated even further to become one of the central concerns of the religion. These teachings warn that if your practice focuses exclusively on detachment, impermanence, and emptiness in the style of the vipassana meditation introduced in the previous chapter, you may wind up in a dry and nihilistic place. To avoid this fate, they advocate that you practice both wisdom and compassion at the same time. The ideal practitioner in Mahayana Buddhism is not the *arahant* who experiences cessation or nirvana through meditative absorption but rather the *bodhisattva* who perceives the emptiness of all phenomena but simultaneously remains intimately connected with this world in order to help others.

Most schools of Buddhism advocate cultivating compassion through specific meditation practices. As I discuss in my book *Buddhish*, Buddhism recognizes four different facets of compassion that can be cultivated independently:

- Loving-kindness (*metta* in Pali): a feeling of universal friendliness, goodwill, and love toward all beings
- Empathetic compassion (*karuna*): a feeling of wanting to remove the suffering experienced by other beings
- Altruistic joy (*mudita*): a feeling of joy at the happiness and success of other beings, untinged by jealousy or pride
- Equanimity (*upekkha*): a feeling of tolerance, peace, and tranquility in the face of annoyances, including those caused by other beings

Using meditation to cultivate these facets of compassion is an effective way to open your heart. On the next few pages I have provided two different meditations from Theravada and Tibetan Buddhist traditions. You can do either of these practices for just a moment when you encounter someone who might need your good wishes, or you can draw it out as long as you want into a formal meditation session—anywhere from a few seconds to a full hour or more.

BOX 5.1: Getting Started with
Compassion Practice (Metta Bhavana)

This is the practice I learned while I was a resident in a monastery in Thailand. It is a common practice in contemporary Theravada Buddhism. It also is highly adaptable. Feel free to adjust the phrases to customize them to your own particular preferences and circumstances.

Start by reviewing the considerations that we talked about in the section on mindfulness in chapter 3 regarding timing and setting. Take a seat in a comfortable chair or on a meditation cushion where you can remain upright but relaxed. Close your eyes and take a few breaths to relax your body.

When you are ready to begin, repeat the following phrases, slowly, pausing after each one to allow it to fully sink in.

> *May I be free from ill will.*
> *May I be free from suffering.*
> *May I be healthy, safe, and happy.*

Having begun with yourself, now imagine these same wishes extending from yourself to reach wider and wider circles of loved ones, such as parents, relatives, friends, teachers, and others. If there are specific people you are concerned about and want to wish well, you can specifically name them.

> *May they be free from ill will.*
> *May they be free from suffering.*
> *May they be healthy, safe, and happy.*

Next, apply these same good wishes to all beings across the planet. At a minimum, include all humans, animals, and insects. If you wish, you can include plants, nature spirits, and other beings of any kind you think might reside on Earth. Whatever global situations are taking place right now, whether wars, famines, or other natural disasters, you can specifically name them.

> *May all the beings of Earth be free from ill will.*
> *May all the beings of Earth be free from suffering.*
> *May all the beings of Earth be healthy, safe, and happy.*

Next, intend for your good wishes to emanate out from your body in all directions—to the north, south, east, west, above and below you—extending to all beings across the planet and beyond to the furthest reaches of the physical universe. Don't exclude anyone from your goodwill!

> *May all beings everywhere be free from ill will.*
> *May all beings everywhere be free from suffering.*
> *May all beings everywhere be healthy, safe, and happy.*

Finally, extend your metta out to the entire cosmos, including all of the realms of existence or other dimensions that may or may not be known. Even the gods, angelic beings, and other divine entities should receive your good wishes.

> *May all beings across the cosmos, known and unknown, be free from*
> *ill will.*
> *May all beings across the cosmos, known and unknown, be free from*
> *suffering.*
> *May all beings across the cosmos, known and unknown, be healthy,*
> *safe, and happy.*

As you practice metta bhavana, pay close attention to any feelings that arise that are indicative of compassion, such as a warmth in your abdomen or a gentleness in your heart area. When such feelings arise, try to sink into them in order to expand the sensations across your body and, eventually, extending beyond your body as well.

Enjoy, and remember that the exercises introduced in this book are only intended to dip your toe into a deeply complex system of practice. If you connect with this practice and think it might be useful for you, it is best to explore this territory with a knowledgeable teacher who can give you personalized guidance. In addition, consult the additional resources at the end of this chapter.

BOX 5.2: Getting Started with Tonglen Practice

Tonglen is a Tibetan meditation that is similar to metta bhavana but which synchronizes visualization and breathing to amplify your good intentions. Again, there are many ways of approaching this practice, and you can customize it as you see fit. For the purposes of illustrating the technique, let's just adapt the meditation in box 5.1.

(continues)

As you go through the meditation in box 5.1, instead of simply intending good-will and focusing on your body sensations, add your breath and some visualization into the mix as well. Each time you focus on a new group of people or beings, imagine that you are breathing in any ill will or suffering they are experiencing. Visualize this as a dark cloud, like smoke or a storm cloud, that you are drawing into your own body.

When you have completed the inhalation, visualize the warm glow of your heart transforming all of the darkness you have taken into your chest into a warm colored light. (Gold is what works for me; you can choose whatever color best symbolizes love and comfort to you.) Now, exhale the light toward the people or beings, bathing them in the warm glow of your compassion. Repeat the breathing cycle for each of the phrases in box 5.1.

For example:

Thinking about all beings to my north:

[Inhale.] *May all beings everywhere be free from ill will.* [Exhale.]

[Inhale.] *May all beings everywhere be free from suffering.* [Exhale.]

[Inhale.] *May all beings everywhere be healthy, safe, and happy.* [Exhale.]

Thinking about all beings to my south:

[Inhale.] *May all beings everywhere be free from ill will.* [Exhale.]

[Inhale.] *May all beings everywhere be free from suffering.* [Exhale.]

[Inhale.] *May all beings everywhere be healthy, safe, and happy.* [Exhale.]

. . . etc.

Again, pay close attention to any sensations such as warmth or tenderness, and visualize breathing into them in order to magnify them.

Enjoy, and remember that the exercises introduced in this book are only in-tended to dip your toe into a deeply complex system of practice. If you connect with this practice and think it might be useful for you, it is best to explore this territory with a knowledgeable teacher who can give you personalized guidance. In addition, consult the additional resources at the end of this chapter.

Phenomenology

As your heart begins to open, you may experience this as a gradual increase over time in your feelings of connectedness and goodwill for others. It is also entirely possible to have a more dramatic opening or even a mystical experience where your being becomes flooded by love, empathy, and joy for all beings.

As with the openings of nondual perception we discussed in the previous chapter, the crucial thing is not the breakthrough experience itself, which will always be temporary. It's the shift in the baseline that takes place after one or more of these experiences that matters. Is there a cumulative change over time leading you in a more heartful direction?

As you deepen into open-heartedness, you will become more and more sensitive to the suffering of people, animals, and all other beings. You'll be more tolerant, patient, and forgiving. It doesn't mean that you'll become meek, passive, or a doormat for others to step on; in fact, you might even become quite outspoken and engaged in fighting injustice.

Compassion can be its own portal to nonduality as the boundary between self and other becomes porous and even dissolves. As your intimacy and connection with others deepens, you may find yourself having a sixth sense for how others are feeling, either picking up on this intuitively or feeling it in your own body. At the deepest levels of openness, the world becomes infused with a feeling of connection and intimacy. All beings seem to be swimming in an ocean of love that is inseparable from who you really are, and that unites all of life into a single heart.

THE SPIRIT WORLD

You may have noticed that the previous exercise mentioned compassion for various divine entities among the many beings that populate the cosmos. Since Asian spiritual traditions developed in societies where people believed in all kinds of unseen beings, there are many practices that involve connecting with or communicating with them.

These practices are different from culture to culture, but there are many commonalities. Generically called *devas, kami, shen*, and other analogous terms, all Asian spiritual traditions recognize a spectrum of spirits, from those we might refer to as "angelic beings" to those we might call "demons." A lot of Asian spirit-based practice is focused on befriending beings on the angelic side of the spectrum and avoiding or pacifying those on the demonic side.

Across Asia, people tend to treat aspects of nature such as mountains, rivers, trees, animals, and so forth as beneficial spirits that can be asked for help and protection. In Japan, for example, gate-like Shinto structures called *torii* mark the entryway to shrines and sacred spaces where people can leave offerings for local nature spirits. In India, the Kumbh Mela festival is a major Hindu pilgrimage taking place every three years that brings over a hundred million people to pay homage to the Ganges River, considered a powerful goddess with the power to bless and protect.

Engagement with the spirits of the dead is also a common feature of Asian religions. In cultures influenced by Confucianism, deceased members of the family are often represented with ancestor tablets, which are placed on an altar within the home or in a temple so that they can receive offerings of fruit, incense, candles, and other gifts from the descendants. In Southeast Asia, Buddhists erect miniature spirit houses behind their homes or places of business, where they leave offerings for wandering ghosts in order to gain good luck and protection. The logic of the spirit house is that it is better to leave offerings for ghosts than to ignore them. If you take care of them they can become your allies, but if you don't they may bother you, haunting your home, causing illness, and bringing other misfortune. This same logic has led to the adoption of various demons into the religion of Buddhism. Across Asia, Buddhist temples frequently feature images of trolls, dragons, and other frightful spirits who have been converted from demonic entities into protectors.

All of the Asian cultures we have been discussing recognize that sometimes malignant spirits can't be controlled so easily with gifts and offerings. They may need to be repelled or removed with talismans, spells, blessed water, or other empowered objects. Across Asia, there are special types of practitioners specializing in such techniques, who are highly valued members of their communities. We are not going to discuss such practices deeply in this book, since these are traditions that require initiation. However, I do want to quickly differentiate between two types of engagement with the spirit world: spirit mediumship, in which the practitioner deals with spirits through activities that they do in *this* world, and shamanism, in which the practitioner travels to the spirit world through some kind of trance state in order to deal with spirits in their own realm. There are a few traditions of shamanism in Korea, Mongolia, parts of Southeast Asia, and elsewhere. However, the vast majority of Asian "spirit doctoring" is of the mediumship variety.

While initiation as a formal practitioner of spirit mediumship or shamanism is rare among Western spiritual seekers and teachers, it is not that unusual for Western practitioners of Asian spirituality to spontaneously experience firsthand contact or communication with the spirit world. Such experiences can unfold in either a mediumistic or shamanic way: either sensing the presence of spirits coming to us or being transported to a different world or dimension where the spirits reside. For some people, these kinds of experiences become more prevalent when they take up more intensive spiritual practice.

We are not concerned in this book with ontological truth claims, so let's not try to pin down whether the spirit world "really exists" or is a projection of our own psychology. However, it is interesting to note that there are different levels of interpretation among Asian traditions on this very question. In Thai Buddhism, for example, spirits are widely considered to be real entities with intentions and agency of their own. In Tibetan Buddhism and other Tantric traditions, on the other hand, spirits are often interpreted metaphorically. Angelic beings are the personifications of our compassion, peacefulness, and other beneficial states of mind, while demons are the personifications of our own fear, anger, or other unprocessed negative emotions.

Whatever they may ultimately be, seeing ghosts, angelic beings, nature spirits, or the spirits of deceased teachers can be a beautiful and highly meaningful experience if it happens to you, or it can be disconcerting and scary. Often, when the experience is positive, it is considered to be a gift, a blessing, or a *siddhi* (a "power") that has opened up as a side effect of spiritual practice. When the experience is negative, it is usually considered to be an undesirable side effect of spiritual practice that should be managed or treated. More severe cases of demonic visitation or possession are in some Buddhist traditions called "meditation sickness" or "wind illness" and are handled with specialized visualizations, breathing exercises, and other interventions.

Whether spirits are real or projections of your own mind, whether you experience the spirit world as a gift or a curse, ultimately, I think that the Mahayana Buddhist approach is the most helpful one. Buddhism holds that there are multiple levels or destinations (*gati*) for rebirth. When you die, in your next life you might be reborn as a human again, but you could also be reborn in a lower destination, as an animal, a ghost, or a being who is trapped in hell. If the karma you accumulated in previous lives is good, you might go to a higher destination and be reborn as an angelic spirit or even a god. Whatever life you are reborn into—even if you become the most exalted god in the cosmos—no being is eternal. You may live for a long time, but eventually you will die and be reborn, the cycle repeating again and again and again until you become enlightened.

Consequently, Mahayana teachings say that whatever type of beings you meet—whether human, animal, or any kind of ghost, spirit, or god—you should understand that they are all equally trapped in the cycle of suffering and rebirth (*samsara*) because of ignorance. Understanding this, you should meet all of the various types of beings, from the lowest to the highest, with compassion and kindness. Engaging with the spirit world in this way can quickly become a path of the heart.

BOX 5.3: Getting Started with
Spirit-Offering Rituals

This kind of practice can be done by anyone, whether you can specifically sense the presence of spirits or unseen beings, or whether you even believe in them. The core of this ritual is to identify a spirit and to make an offering of some kind to it. It may be best to begin with an ancestor of yours, the sun or moon, or a prominent nature spirit in the place where you live (if you live by a body of water, a mountain, or a forest, for example). The first time you do it, you should choose a spirit that brings up a lot of positive emotions for you, with which the relationship is not complicated or difficult and the spirit is an unambiguously beneficial influence.

This offering ritual can be done anytime and anywhere, but it can also gain a certain amount of charge or poignancy if done at a particular place or time. For example, you can honor the spirit of a lake when simply imagining the lake, but you might feel more resonance when you are actually standing on the shore. Likewise, you can honor the moon anytime, but it may be more resonant to do so at night, and perhaps even more so when you are bathed in the light of the full moon. If you are working with an ancestor, maybe do the ritual on their birthday, the anniversary of their passing away, or another significant date. When you are starting out in this kind of practice, it is a good idea to intentionally try to maximize the resonance you feel when doing your offering. The more significance you can generate via the setting, the better.

The offering that you give during the ritual also should be poignant and meaningful. The perfect offering for the spirit of my deceased father, for example, would be a small glass of Johnnie Walker Black Label whiskey and some tobacco, both of which he loved when he was alive. But I would definitely not offer that to the spirit of my deceased vipassana meditation teacher, who never drank or smoked and in fact looked down upon those as bad habits.

What do you offer the spirit of the sun or moon, or of a lake or mountain? There are traditions that prescribe what you offer, but I prefer to use intuition as my guide. You might offer a candle to the sun, giving fire to fire. You might offer a bowl of water to the moon, catching the moonlight in the reflection of the water. Be creative and tap into something that is resonant for you.

When you are ready to perform the offering, stand facing the spirit you are addressing (or imagine it before you) while holding your offering. Speak out loud or very clearly say the words in your mind, focusing on expressing goodwill and

(continues)

kindness toward the spirit. You may say something like the following, or make up your own phrases that are meaningful to you:

Hello, I am [your name]. I am here to make an offering to you, to symbolize my respect for you and my good wishes. Thank you for your existence, your protection, and your blessings. I recognize you and want to be in good relationship with you. I am open to any response that you may wish to make, or anything you wish to communicate to me.

Place the offering as if giving it to the spirit. Now, sit or stand silently for five to ten minutes. Partially, this is to allow some time for the spirit to consume or appreciate the offering. Also, this is a moment for you to see if there is any response to your gift.

Don't expect the spirit to take shape in front of you and speak out loud in human language. That could happen, but the response to your gift, if any, will almost always be much more subtle. It might be a faint smell on the breeze, a distant sound, a vision, thought, or feeling. The trick to receiving the response is to quietly attend to your senses in a way that is open to and curious about whatever might happen. If you do sense something, just observe calmly without jumping too quickly to interpret it.

Remember not to get hung up on the ontological question of whether these communications are coming from a separate entity with its own mind or if they are bubbling up from your own unconscious. Either way, this ritual is about opening your heart, not increasing your thinking, so focus on the feelings and emotions involved in your exchanges with the spirits regardless of what you think might be "really" going on.

When you are finished, discard any organic material in your offering by burying it, pouring it out, or placing it on the earth. Plastic, glass, and other materials should be recycled or reused as appropriate.

Note that this is not about communicating with ghosts or spirits in order to get answers to your questions, to predict the future, to get winning lottery numbers, or whatever. It's not about praying to gods to fulfill the desires or wishes you might have. It's about intuiting that there is much more to reality than we can perceive with the conventional senses, and that much more of it is conscious than we might have originally suspected.

Phenomenology

Regardless of what you believe, if you conduct spirit offering rituals frequently, it will likely begin to have an effect on how you perceive trees, animals, features of the landscape, and other living aspects of nature. You may also begin to feel that certain objects you previously thought of as "inanimate" have a kind of sentience or consciousness. You may gratefully recognize the presence of the ancestors in everything you do and are today. You may come to see the universe as teeming with angelic and ghostly forces, all of whom can hear and receive your good wishes. You may begin to see the world as a whole panoply of conscious beings, who you greet with compassion and kindness.

Dwelling in a place where we are constantly wishing all seen and unseen entities to be well, we evolve into an open-hearted being who radiates kindness throughout the multidimensional cosmos. Eventually, over time, as your ability to discern the unseen world gets better and better, you may find yourself having a relationship that involves two-way communication. You may receive messages from unseen beings, or perhaps receive unexpected blessings that seem to manifest out of nowhere. The spirit world responds to your kindness and compassion, and your life becomes one of increasing harmony and intimacy with all of manifest reality.

DEVOTION

Devotion is another major feature of Asian spirituality that has a direct role in opening the heart. As mentioned in a previous section, one of the main three forms of Hindu spiritual discipline is Bhakti Yoga, the path of devotion. Bhakti typically refers to the emotionally engaged reverence for specific deities. As mentioned previously, Hinduism recognizes a whole range of deities, including Shiva, Vishnu, Hanuman, Ganesh, Rama, Krishna, Durga, Kali, Lakshmi, and Sarasvati, among many others.

Most Buddhists also practice devotion for deities. In Theravada, this devotion is usually directed just at one Buddha (named

Siddhartha Gautama or, in some traditions, Shakyamuni). Mahayana Buddhism, on the other hand, recognizes multiple Buddhas, including the Medicine Buddha and Amitabha Buddha, as well as powerful celestial bodhisattvas such as Guanyin, Tara, Maitreya, Mañjushri, and Vajrapani. All forms of Buddhism also pay homage to divinized master teachers such as Budai, Padmasambhava, Somdet To, and Tsongkhapa. Buddhist traditions additionally incorporate what are sometimes called "wrathful deities," powerful demons who have been converted to Buddhism. In Tibetan Buddhism, this class of deities includes most notably Mahakala and Palden Lhamo, two ferocious-looking monsters who are actually revered as protectors of the faith (*dharmapala*).

Western spiritual explorers are typically more interested in meditation than in devotion to deities. However, serious engagement with certain forms of Hinduism and Buddhism typically requires Western practitioners to be devout. In addition to their devotion to deities, Asian traditions often place a high value on honoring teachers, a practice often referred to as "guru yoga." Whatever the path looks like, making serious progress on the journey toward enlightenment in pretty much all Asian forms of spirituality is usually said to be exceedingly difficult or impossible without wholeheartedly submitting to the guidance of a teacher.

Partially, the importance of the teacher rests on the need for customized, individualized instruction. Each of the systems we have considered in this book includes a wide range of different meditations, inquiries, and other practices, and it is important to know how and when it is appropriate to use each of them in order to streamline one's spiritual development. It is often said that the individual practitioner is their own worst teacher, since they will likely gravitate toward what is most comfortable or easy instead of what is most helpful or necessary in the moment. It is probably most efficient to get personalized advice from someone who has been down the path many times in the past, who knows how to navigate the way and how to avoid the obstacles.

Aside from knowledgeable guidance, another reason why Asian spiritual traditions say that teachers are necessary is because of a certain intangible power they can transmit to their students. This transmission is spoken about in different ways in different systems. Hindu practitioners, for example, talk about *shaktipat*, a shot of energy that a practitioner receives by coming in contact with an enlightened teacher or individual. One example of a teacher who gives such blessings whom many Western spiritual explorers will know is Mata Amritanandamayi Devi, fondly known by her followers as "the hugging saint" or simply Amma ("Mother"). Amma is famous for giving *shaktipat* through the act of hugging, and wherever she goes throngs of people line up to receive her blessing. According to *Wikipedia*, at the time of this writing, she has hugged over thirty-three million people all around the world throughout her three-decades long career.

Other Hindu gurus give *shaktipat* in different ways: by touch, by a look, by some words or other utterances. In the same way, practitioners of East Asian martial arts may receive a transmission of qi or ki from their teacher in order to light up their own energy body. Practitioners of Tibetan Buddhism, on the other hand, seek out "empowerments" from their teachers through rituals that open up specific kinds of spiritual results. The recipient of an empowerment often has to perform certain rituals or observe particular taboos in order to maintain the effectiveness of the empowerment.

While all of the transmissions discussed so far can be given to lower-level practitioners, in Zen, "dharma transmission" is reserved until a student has reached a certain level of accomplishment in meditation and is ready to be honored and publicly recognized. Transmissions in Zen are an important part of the tradition's focus on lineage and play a role in certifying or endorsing the student as legitimately having received and understood the dharma. You cannot become a legitimate Zen teacher without this transmission or without being formally recognized by a lineage.

In all of these ways, respect for teachers, lineage, and transmission is a universal feature of Asian spirituality. However, in Hinduism and Vajrayana Buddhism this respect often manifests as a form of intense ritual and emotional devotion toward the guru. In the process, human teachers are elevated into quasi or literal deities in their own right. The way that some practitioners of neo-Advaita talk about Ramana Maharshi or that some practitioners of Buddhism talk about the Dalai Lama, for example, are essentially indistinguishable from deity worship.

Phenomenology

The book you are holding in your hand is a guidebook for people who are interested in exploring spirituality, not in becoming fervent devotees of any particular teacher or sect. Therefore, in introducing the surrender ritual in box 5.4, I am emphatically not suggesting you surrender your own judgment or discernment about what is right for you. And I certainly don't mean for you to surrender your autonomy, allowing a teacher or organization to tell you what to do.

However, all of the types of devotion discussed in this section, whether to deities or teachers, can contribute to opening the heart. They all can lead you beyond your small, limited sense of self and can connect you with something larger and more intimate than your everyday relationships. When you are completely devoted to a teacher and surrender yourself completely to their guidance, they potentially may lead you into territory that you could not have possibly traversed on your own.

Perhaps you are familiar with the Christian concept of "Thy will be done" or the Islamic equivalent "In sha'Allah"? In Buddhism, a similar idea is expressed with the notion of "taking refuge" in the Buddha, dharma, and sangha. In Hinduism, they talk about *sharanagati*, or total surrender to the divine. The shared notion here is to give up the idea that our lives are under the control of our little egos with all of their desires and neuroses. To cultivate a sense that we are cared for and guided by benevolent forces.

BOX 5.4: Getting Started with a Surrender Ritual

This kind of practice can be done by anyone, regardless of your beliefs. The intention is not to turn you into a devotee of a particular religion. As with the practice introduced in the previous section, the ontological questions of whether spirits or gods exist does not concern us. The intention of this practice is not to figure out what's "really" going on but rather to simply open our hearts beyond the limits of the small separate self.

As with the previous offering ceremony, pay attention to increasing the resonance through the setting and timing of your ritual. One way of maximizing its poignancy is through the creation of an altar space. An altar is simply a dedicated space where you skillfully array a number of symbols to evoke deeper feelings. You can use any shelf, table, or other flat surface in your home or place of work, so long as it is exclusively used for ritual practices. The more you can separate the space from your ordinary mundane activities, the better.

In the middle of the space, directly facing you, place an image, statue, drawing, or other symbolic representation of the "spiritual guide" you feel has the most spiritual wisdom and compassion of all. Choose an image that represents the highest version of enlightenment you can possibly conceive of—whether that's a spiritual leader, a deity, or some kind of abstract symbol, like the yin-yang sign or OM written in Sanskrit.

You can place other objects on the altar that support or highlight the importance and emotional resonance of this central image. Some typical items on Asian spiritual practitioners' altars include candles, incense, and flowers, usually arranged symmetrically. However, don't clutter your altar with things that are tangential to your own practice. Only objects that have a deep spiritual meaning for you or that serve a specific purpose in your ritual should be placed here.

You might begin your ritual by lighting candles or incense, and you might include some kind of offering or gift giving for the central image, such as we discussed in the previous exercise. After these preliminaries, the heart of this particular ritual is to surrender control over our lives and, in particular, over our spiritual development. You might do this by repeating a phrase like this one:

I surrender my life and my spiritual path to [insert]. I am not able to foresee the most beneficial course of action, and I am not able to know in advance the outcomes of any decision I make. Please teach me, guide me, and keep me safe on my journey. I give all control over to you.

(continues)

Repeat your phrase slowly, paying attention to any response or reaction that you have. If you experience any fear, doubt, or other distracting thoughts or feelings arising, surrender these as well:

I surrender my fear to you.
I surrender my doubt to you.

If you feel yourself clinging to any objects or aspects of your life that you are especially attached to, surrender these as well:

I surrender my attachment to [insert] to you.

Keep going like this for five to ten minutes, identifying any resistance that arises and surrendering it. You may wish to finish with a few words of gratitude for your spiritual guide and some metta for yourself.

There can be a lot of fear that arises when we think about surrendering control. But if you open your heart instead of thinking about it, you might discover a natural ease and a flow to everything. Things just fall into place perfectly, and the universe delivers to you precisely what is needed in the moment. By surrendering the ego's desire to control our lives, we come to feel in touch with our deepest calling, that we are living out our destiny, our Tao, our soul's mission on Earth. (Your objective circumstances may not be any different: I'm talking about how you feel.)

At the deepest levels of surrender, you may no longer experience free will, agency, or intentionality. By letting go of micromanaging our experience at every moment, it seems as if life is instead at every moment guided by divine grace.

DETOURS ON THE PATH

Like the transformation of perception, the opening of the heart can happen gradually over time with more stability and predictability, or it can happen suddenly and surprisingly. As with all advanced spiritual practices, engaging with the practices discussed in this chapter might lead to a breakthrough or mystical experience with dramatic and potentially destabilizing effects. Such experiences might include suddenly being completely overwhelmed with divine love, merging with a deity and losing your sense of self entirely, being spontaneously transported to a different dimension or to a world of spirits, or experiencing unexpected contact with various spiritual entities. These experiences can range from extremely pleasant to absolutely terrifying. However they show up, they can destabilize one's sense of reality and take some time to get used to. Again, they are rare, but just knowing that these kinds of things may happen and that they are temporary can be helpful.

Keep in mind that unexpected things can also occur even as your heart opens more slowly. One of the most common side effects of an open heart is viscerally feeling the people around you, like your own body is mirroring the emotions of people nearby. Extreme openness can sometimes lead to intense feelings of sadness or pain, as if you are taking on the suffering of the entire world. People with very open hearts can be easily overwhelmed by encounters with certain people, tragedies in the news, violent TV shows, and other occasions where they pick up on the feelings of others. People who are particularly prone to experiencing spirits might feel unpleasant "vibes" associated with places or objects, or they may feel threatened or overwhelmed by certain unseen entities or energies on occasion.

All of these situations require a special kind of discernment to be able to clearly separate out what is "yours" versus what is "theirs." There are also specific practices that can help you to process what is happening and shield you against picking up so many stray vibes and spirits. (The grounding exercises introduced in chapter 3 are particularly helpful in this regard.) In addition, as with all unexpected outcomes, reducing the intensity of your spiritual practices or switching to different types of spiritual activities can help resolve most issues. As always, there are resources and assistance if you feel that you need them at the end of the chapter 3.

Another big potential downside to the devotional aspects of spirituality introduced in this chapter is getting entangled with a problematic teacher. In a well-functioning spiritual community, the reliance on teachers for instruction and empowerment should operate in a healthy way that is supportive for all students. However, in real life, devotion for teachers often can become quite dysfunctional, leading to a disease that I call "guruitis."

In my view, guruitis is common because Asian spiritual communities are too often structured in ways that encourage members to have complete dependency on teachers while the teachers are held up as perfectly enlightened beings who can do no wrong. The ideas of devotion, transmission, and surrender I talked about in this chapter continually reinforce the idea that lower-level practitioners are powerless, that they are ignorant, and that they cannot know what is best for them. Meanwhile, the guru is being presented as a model of perfection, the pinnacle of human achievement, perhaps even a godlike superhuman. What could possibly go wrong?

Perhaps this arrangement worked better in premodern times or perhaps it's a better fit for Asian cultures. Who knows? Here in the modern West, guruitis takes shape as a kind of toxic hypnosis that infects participants in many kinds of spiritual environments. Seekers fall under a guru's spell and give away their individuality, their agency, and their power. They become sock puppets, repeating the words of their tradition without thinking for themselves. They make excuses for their guru's questionable and abusive behaviors, become blinded to inconsistencies in the guru's teachings, and withdraw from friends or family who don't share their devotion or beliefs. In the extreme, guruitis can lead to fanaticism or even cult-like behaviors.

There have been too many examples of guruitis in recent decades to even begin to list them all here. But, for some examples, just look up the scandals surrounding Maezumi Roshi (1931–1995), Sogyal Rinpoche (1947–2019), and Bikram Choudhury (1944–). Gurus and teachers of all types have been convicted or accused of sexually harassing their students, coercing them financially, manipulating them psychologically, and abusing power for their own ends. In the US, these kinds of events have especially affected Hindu, Tibetan Buddhist, and Zen communities, and they almost always have involved male teachers. But there is no branch of Asian spiritual traditions and no kind of community that has been untouched by this disease.

I personally have never made a serious commitment to a particular spiritual community or teacher for any length of time, in large part because of my own ingrained skepticism toward authority figures. I have always preferred to go it alone, to guide my own spiritual path—willing to take the risk that I wouldn't progress as much as I otherwise might under the direction of a teacher. But that's my choice. You must make your own. If you feel differently and wish to join up with a group, we are fortunate that, these days, a ton of information can be found with a simple Google search. There is now no excuse for not having done your homework, for not giving the teachers you are considering a full and proper vetting.

If you do choose to join a particular community or follow a particular guru, I think it is equally important to constantly remind yourself to keep your eyes wide open as you move forward. Be highly suspicious of any organization or teacher that seems as if they are asking you to give away your own autonomy or agency—even if this is being couched in inspirational spiritual language. You should especially be on the lookout for anyone who asks for financial commitments or sexual favors of any kind, as these kinds of transactions simply do not belong in a spiritual setting. If other people in the community report to you that they are being abused in some way, or if any of your loved ones express concern for your well-being based on your recent behaviors, these are also huge red flags. Always use common sense and maintain a healthy skepticism. And constantly keep questioning if you are being skillfully guided or if you are being hypnotized or manipulated.

As in the previous chapter, the approaches discussed here are complex, ancient systems of practice with many variations. My intention is to give you starting points for further exploration and investigation. As usual, some further resources are provided below to help you connect with resources for deeper practice. There are many Asian spiritual practices related to opening the heart that are not mentioned in this chapter. Many of these have been omitted because they cross a line from the spiritually exploratory to the overtly religious. The resources I recommend contain additional information about other practices not covered here.

BOX 5.5: Additional Resources for Exploring the Heart

PODCASTS

- *Buddha at the Gas Pump*—Interviews with spiritual teachers of all kinds. Keyword-search the past episodes to find teachers affiliated with different approaches mentioned in this chapter, and then listen to the interviews to sample their teachings.

BOOKS

- Sharon Salzberg, *Lovingkindness: The Revolutionary Art of Happiness*— A classic introduction to Buddhist compassion practice
- Thich Naht Hanh, *Cultivating the Mind of Love*—An exploration of the role of love in Buddhist spirituality
- Chöying Khandro, *Dakini Journey in the Contemporary World*—Tibetan Buddhist perspectives on goddesses and other feminine spirits
- Graphic novels published by Amar Chitra Katha—A series of accessible, illustrated retellings of the myths of many popular Hindu deities
- Matthew D. Remski, *Practice and All Is Coming: Abuse, Cult Dynamics, and Healing in Yoga and Beyond*—A book about the underlying dynamics that lead to abuse in teacher-student relationships

CHAPTER 6

EXPLORING THE ENERGY BODY

Y ou may have noticed that the body was mostly missing from the previous two chapters. We did discuss certain forms of meditation that took the breath or body sensations as meditation objects. However, at the end of the day, those meditations were aiming to evoke a shift in your perception, not necessarily to transform your experience of embodiment. Likewise, certain forms of the heart-opening practice I introduced involve using your breath (as is the case with tonglen) or using your body in particular ways (as with ritual gestures). However, again, these practices are aiming to change your sense of presence and engagement with the world, not specifically of your body. The techniques introduced in this chapter, on the other hand, are methods of sparking spiritual transformation that prioritize the body per se.

I learned firsthand the difference between approaches that center the body versus those that don't when I was in my twenties. In Thailand, I was spending a lot of time at Theravada Buddhist meditation centers and monasteries. In these settings, we did a ton of seated meditation and chanting—sometimes up to ten hours per day—which put a brutal toll on my knees and back. We slept little, waking up at 4 or 5 a.m. We also severely restricted our diet, eating food only until noon and then fasting for the rest of the day. Most afternoons, the monks and fellow meditators loaded up on caffeine and sugar to get enough energy to make it through the rest of the day. Other than some manual labor to maintain the monastic buildings and grounds, we never did physical exercise of any kind. In fact, physical cultivation methods such as stretching and movement practices were expressly forbidden in most of those settings. The focus was primarily on transforming perception (and sometimes on opening the heart). Cultivating the body in any way was seen as a distraction and a waste of time. Even just tending to its needs in a way you or I might consider normal (like taking an afternoon siesta, for example) was ridiculed as "coddling" or "indulging" the body.

However, during those same years I was in Asia, I also spent several months at yoga ashrams both in Southern India and in the foothills of the Himalayas. The contrast was striking. In this type of setting, we also did seated meditation and chanting but only for two to three hours per day. We also engaged in three to four hours of guided Hathayoga practice each day. We ate breakfast, lunch, and dinner: three square meals designed around the principles of sattvic eating (that is, gentle for your digestion) and Ayurvedic medicine (attuning the diet to the seasons for optimal physical health).

These two types of settings were equally devoted to spiritual practice, but the difference between how I felt physically in them was stark and made a lasting impression on me. For the rest of my life, I have always approached spirituality in a way that has shown care and compassion for my body.

This being said, in this chapter, when I say body, I don't just mean the material body of muscles, bones, organs, and so forth. Although maintaining the body's physical health and well-being is of extreme importance, the techniques introduced here are not simply focusing on taking care of the body at the physical level. Nor are these practices about gaining strength, flexibility, or athletic endurance—although such things may happen as side effects of more body-oriented forms of spiritual practice. The methods I'm talking about in this chapter specifically involve cultivating the underlying "energy body." I'm sure you're aware that energy is an important part of some Asian approaches, and we've already mentioned it a few times, but let's dig into that topic a bit in order to be sure we're all on the same page.

WHAT IS ENERGY?

Science tells us that our bodies are solid objects made of tissues, fluids, and other biological material. But phenomenologically, it's a completely different story, isn't it?

If you pay close attention to your experience of what it feels like to have a body, sometimes it does feel like a physical mass. For example, if you put your attention on your legs right now, you may feel that they have a solid corporeal presence. You may feel pressure, volume, and weight. Your body may feel like a clump of earth or clay, being held by gravity and taking up space.

But the body is probably not always so solid in your actual experience. When you feel a hunger pang, for example, it doesn't seem like your abdomen is a solid mass of flesh. If you ignore what you know theoretically and just close your eyes and focus on the actual phenomenology of your bodily experience, doesn't it feel more like a little prickly, bubbly sensation floating within empty space? Likewise, the feeling of being startled doesn't feel solid either. Isn't it more like a sudden electric shock, followed by an icy cloud of tingles?

If you pay attention, I think you'll find that there are many occasions when the solidity of your body seems to disappear altogether. Have you ever slipped into a hot tub and felt how the shape and form of your body seem to melt away into a pool of buttery warmth? Or experienced an orgasm where the contours of your body were obliterated by waves of sparkles? Or a huge sneeze where it feels that your entire body has just exploded like a supernova?

The language I'm using here is suggestive and metaphorical because we don't really have in English a specific vocabulary to speak about the felt bodily experiences of such events. You could grasp intuitively what I'm trying to convey, but wouldn't communicating about this be much easier if our culture had developed terminology to refer to all of these kinds of phenomena? Well, as it turns out, Asian cultures have developed such a vocabulary.

I've already talked about the Chinese term *qi*, the word that is used in so many different ways in East Asian cultures to refer to dynamism and movement. One of the main ways that qi is used is as a name for the whole field of body sensations. Indian Tantric systems also developed a word that encompasses these kinds of phenomena: *prana*.

Westerners often translate both qi and prana using the English word *energy*, and it can be helpful to use that word to explain certain Asian concepts that are hard to express otherwise in English. However, the word itself can also be misleading. Hearing talk about "bodily energy" or the "energy body" is likely to make many people think there is some subtle, esoteric, invisible aura or force that only those who are really "in the know" can perceive. Maybe you think you have to take an expensive seminar in order to be able to feel energy, or maybe you feel that you're never going to get it, or maybe you just have written all of this off as woo-woo nonsense.

Of course, Chinese and Indian theory around qi and prana gets much more complicated than I am able to get into in this brief introduction. There are complex maps of Chinese "meridians" and Indian *nadis* that were historically developed in order to understand the movements of qi and prana in the human bodies for spiritual and medical purposes. But for our present purposes here in this chapter, instead of digging deeply into all the theory, let's just cut to the chase. I'll put it succinctly like this: everyone is already perfectly capable of experiencing qi or prana, and you are already doing so all day long. "My qi feels solid," "my qi feels spacious," "my prana feels collected," "my prana feels dissipated": all of these are just culturally specific ways of efficiently communicating the kinds of feelings that I was talking about above. They are ways of speaking about the normal human felt experience of being in a body—the phenomenology of body sensations.

Body-centered Asian practices like yoga, tai chi, qigong, and others that we will discuss in this chapter are key tools for spiritual development because they provide ways of becoming more aware of the fluctuations of qi and prana. That is to say, they are ways of moving beyond thinking about your body in terms of a big solid block of flesh and instead experiencing it as a boundless field pulsating with sensory phenomena. The practices introduced in this chapter each in their own way involve using the combination of movement, breathing, and awareness in order to open us up to experiencing this field of sensations. They also all offer ways to enhance the mobility, flow, and subtlety of those sensations.

The more you engage with the forms of energy practice introduced here, the less you'll feel confined to a gross, material, physical body, and the more you'll feel like your body is vibrant, expansive, and spacious. Experiencing your body in this way is quite liberating. If you're thinking about your body as a lump of flesh, then when you experience an unpleasant sensation, it feels solid and localized. But if you experience your body as an open field of fluctuating phenomena, then an unpleasant sensation arising here or there isn't such a big deal. It's not that unpleasant stimuli go away, but they are able to flow through the field much more easily. This means that unpleasant feelings associated with emotions, memories, interactions with others, and other kinds of events in your life can freely arise, move about, and then dissipate without becoming fixated or stuck.

Over time, you may notice some physical changes from engaging in the practices outlined in this chapter. You may become healthier, more flexible, have better immunity, or experience other kinds of physiological benefits. You'll also notice that an energetically free and open body feels more pleasurable to inhabit than one that is energetically blocky and thick. However, we're interested in opening the energy body not because of these physical or emotional benefits but because of the positive effect this will have on our spiritual growth. Traditionally, these practices are said to lead to the transformation of the gross physical body into an enlightened spiritual body. The enlightened body is the highest goal of many systems of Asian spiritual practice. It is called the "body of light" in certain forms of Hindu Tantra, the "rainbow body" in Tibetan Buddhism, and the "immortal body" in Taoism.

MOVING MEDITATION

Of the Asian spiritual practices that primarily focus on cultivating the energy body, some are more well-known in the West than others. You have likely heard of yoga, tai chi, and qigong. Less common, but becoming more so in recent years, are Tibetan practices related to yoga that are called "magical movements" or "yantra yoga" (*trul khor* or *tsa lung trul khor*) and Taoist forms of cultivation called "internal work" (*neigong*) or "internal alchemy" (*neidan*). I think of all of these as varieties of "moving meditation." That isn't a traditional name for these practices but an English term that is meant to highlight how movement, breathing, and awareness are the core of each of them.

The three most popular forms of moving meditation in the West—yoga, tai chi, and qigong—are distinct in how they approach energy cultivation. Each of these systems developed a number of divergent schools or styles. In chapter 2, I briefly gave an overview of the evolution of these arts from the ancient to modern periods. But I didn't talk about the similarities and differences between them in practice.

Traditional yoga primarily involves putting the body into static postures that you hold steady while you breathe deeply and relax into them. In contrast, qigong requires you to continually move, coordinating your breath with movements you repeat over and over. Whereas yoga postures tend to involve 45 degree, 90 degree, and 180 degree angles, qigong's motions tend to be more circular. Tai chi, on the other hand, is essentially a martial art form that has been dramatically slowed down. It combines both angular and circular movements in a continual flow that also synchronizes with the breathing. Tai chi involves memorizing a sequence consisting of dozens of complex movements. While yoga and qigong are fully customizable for the individual, a tai chi routine is done in the same way and in a fixed order by all students of the system.

(Although this may be obvious, I think I should add a note here just to be certain to clarify that, in this chapter, when I say "yoga," I am not referring to the modern athletic forms of yoga that you might find at the gym or local health studio. Cultivation of the energy body has nothing to do with huffing and puffing through a series of *chaturangas* so you can look good in your yoga pants! Nor does it have anything to do with stretching your hamstrings to cross-train for your weightlifting workout. That kind of yoga is perfectly fine if that's what you prefer as an exercise routine. But traditional yoga is not about fitness. It's not even actually about the physical body. Like all of the practices discussed in this chapter, the reason for doing asanas, or body postures, in yoga is to open up the energy body for optimal spiritual development.)

Phenomenology

When you are first learning any one of these systems of moving meditation, you are primarily focused on memorizing the movements and correcting your alignment. During this phase, if you are engaging in these exercises in a serious way, you'll likely experience some physical shifts in your body as certain muscles become stronger, as others become more flexible, and as your whole body adjusts to the new regimen.

In my experience, this phase takes at least six months of daily practice. Don't get impatient. If you think about it, this length of time is really the same for learning any new embodied skill: You could go out for a run today if you wanted to, but how many months of daily running would it take for you to develop the body of a runner? Or if you started guitar lessons today, how long would it take for you to develop the nimble fingers of a guitarist?

It takes time, but once your body has physically acclimated to the practice, the movements become effortless, like second nature. When there are no catches or kinks in your physical performance, your mind no longer needs to constantly dwell on what to do or how to do it. Then your body and mind can come together naturally in sync with your movements and breath.

As your mind settles in, it enjoys and appreciates your body sensations at subtler and subtler levels. Your awareness becomes more and more attuned to feelings of fluidity and ease. You begin to apprehend flow, openness, and freedom within the body. There can be a faint sense of bliss, like a warm stream of water or a cool electric current running along your skin and deeper inside your body. There can be waves of joyful pleasure, like mini orgasms rippling across your sensory field.

At a certain point, the solidity of your body begins to dissolve. Whether it happens quickly or gradually, eventually the boundaries of your body may disappear altogether, leaving just a field of subtle sensations dancing in empty space. Your body sensations feel like stars and galaxies in the night sky. Here, you find yet another portal to nonduality. The separate bodily self you have long identified with is gone, and you experience yourself as stardust gently vibrating and sparkling in the void.

BOX 6.1: Getting Started with Moving Meditation

Yoga, qigong, and tai chi are all complex systems of practice that take many years of instruction and guidance to cultivate. It is difficult to introduce any single practice here in a way that could give you an authentic taste of these systems in a bite-sized morsel.

That being said, I think the best approach is to go back to two of the practices introduced in exercises 3.2 and 3.3, corpse pose and post stance. When I introduced these previously, I focused on their role in helping you feel grounded and relaxed. That is to say, I focused on the physical dimension of these exercises.

Let's return to the same exercises with a different mindset, focused on energy. Plan on practicing either corpse pose or post stance (or both) for ten to fifteen minutes at least twice per day. If you've already been practicing these postures and breathing methods regularly for any length of time, you may already know what needs to be done physically and can start to tune into the more subtle aspects straight away. If you haven't practiced them yet, spend some time focusing on the instructions given in chapter 3, adjusting your alignment until the exercises feel like they are natural and easeful for you.

When you are ready to focus on the subtler aspects, do the postures and breathing the same way you have always done, but now let go of thinking about the physical dimension of the exercise. Never mind about posture or alignment. Just allow your awareness to settle into the sensations that you feel. You might especially focus on the sensations in your lower abdomen below your belly button, your chest area, or the midpoint inside your skull. These are all *dantians*, or highly sensitive areas that serve as gateways to the body's subtler energies, which I will discuss later on in this chapter.

Let go of any tension you feel in these areas. Now, gently attune to how these areas feel as you breathe deeply into your posture. Gently attune to how your breath is giving your internal organs a rhythmic massage. Gently attune to how your pelvis and spine undulate with each breath. This isn't about maintaining laser-like focus on those areas of your body; it's more like appreciating and relishing the sensations that are arising.

Now, ever so slightly, start making very subtle movements that accentuate the movements your body is making naturally. With each in-breath, gently exaggerate the expansion of your torso that's already taking place. With each out-breath, gently exaggerate the contraction. With each in-breath, gently exaggerate the forward tilt of your pelvis and arch in your spine that is already taking place. With each out-breath, gently exaggerate the backward tilt and straightening.

As you do these movements, sink into your body sensations deeper and deeper, like you are sinking into a bubble bath or a hot tub. Sense if it feels better to make your movements bigger, smaller, slower, or faster. Don't rush this practice. Enjoy discovering whatever your body most prefers for as long as you wish. Allow your body to move however it wants or needs to in order to maximize the feeling of pleasure as you dissolve into a swirl of warm, bubbly, sensory bliss.

When you are finished, see if you perceive a difference in your emotions, attention, and physical energy levels as you go about the rest of your day.

SACRED SEXUALITY

Frank discussions of sexuality are relatively rare in Western books about Asian spiritual traditions. There are countless popular books about spirituality that talk about virtually all aspects of life, but often sex is conspicuously ignored. In my opinion, our general prejudice against mixing sex and spirituality in Western culture is most likely a product of centuries of sexual repression under the influence of Christianity.

To be fair, Asian traditions that are dismissive of the body tend to marginalize sexuality every bit as much as Christianity. For example, virtually all traditions of Buddhism require ordained monastics to be completely celibate. The monastic rules, known as the *vinaya*, often prescribe severe punishments for any type of sex or masturbation by monastics, or even for being alone with a member of the opposite sex. Since it traditionally would only have been in a monastic setting that you would deeply engage with meditation, the reality is that historical people essentially had to choose either to be a meditator or to be sexually active. A similar choice was required in many forms of Hinduism, where serious practitioners must take vows of chastity known as *brahmacharya*.

As a scholar of the history of Buddhism, I have had the opportunity to read numerous Buddhist scriptures. I have found that many of these writings not only prescribe complete sexual abstinence but also go out of their way to demonize sex. Such texts frequently paint a grotesque picture of this realm of human life in ways that have always struck me as repressive and misogynistic. Meditations where you visualize male and female sexual organs as infested with worm-like parasites, for example, or discourses equating the menstrual cycle to poison and pollution.

Be that as it may, there are several spiritual traditions in Asia that have had a completely different tone when it comes to this subject. Both Taoism and Chinese medicine, for example, see sex as natural, enjoyable, and having an overall positive influence on health. So do certain Tantric traditions. Rather than repress sexuality, these systems embrace it and mobilize it as part of the spiritual journey to enlightenment.

I feel like I need to pause to introduce a note of clarification at this point. In the West, the word Tantra has been misappropriated and its meaning has been almost completely distorted. I thus want to make a clear distinction here between incorporating sexuality into one's spiritual practice on the one hand and practicing techniques that are merely focused on maximizing one's sexual prowess, pleasure, or fertility on the other. While some Asian traditions

BOX 6.2: Getting Started with Meditation on Erotic Bliss

Lie on your back in the corpse pose. Begin by doing the "moving meditation" exercise presented in the previous section (box 6.1). You'll want to follow all of the instructions presented there for a good five to ten minutes before proceeding.

When you feel comfortably submersed in a bubble bath of sensations, bend your knees and place a bolster or cushion underneath your legs to support them. Let your legs gently fall open to the sides. In this position, continue to breathe and sense your body's subtle movements and energy flows. Pay particular attention to the sensations in your lower abdomen below your navel as well as your genitals.

This area of your body is able to produce a significant amount of blissful energy without even touching it. These sensations have an erotic quality to them, but this is not about building sexual tension. It's not about feeling "sexy" or "horny." See if you can find the right combination of breath, awareness, and gentle movement that spontaneously produces gentle erotic pleasure that originates in this area and ripples throughout your body. Relax, be patient, and enjoy this exploration for as long as you like.

If you feel moved, you can either touch your genitals yourself or explore this practice with a beloved partner. If you do, try to maintain a non-goal-oriented attitude. This is a meditation, so relax into the sensations rather than building pressure. Make a point of not orgasming. Or do so but make a point of putting it off for as long as possible while you feel every single sparkle of energy that arises.

However you practice it, imagine that the blissful sensations you're generating in this exercise are nourishing your entire body, making you more energized, healthy, alert, awake, and compassionate. Then, see if you perceive a difference in your emotions, attention, and physical energy levels as you go about the rest of your day.

focus on the latter—such as the famous *Kama Sutra* from India and premodern *shunga* pornography from Japan—if there is no higher spiritual goal of true transformation or transcendence behind the practice, then properly speaking, it's not Tantra. In this section, I am concerned only with Tantric approaches to sexuality that are intended to enhance spiritual cultivation.

So, exactly how does sexuality fit into spirituality? In the last section, we discussed how engaging in moving meditation can transform your experience of your body from a solid lump of flesh into a sparkling field of bliss. Well, if breathing and movement can produce such an effect, it may not be surprising to hear that sexuality can do so as well. In fact, for many people, sexual activity can be one of the most effective routes to discovering and working with the energy body.

However, it's important to note that when I say "sexual activity," I am talking about something different than conventional sex or masturbation. For most people, sex is about building up a large amount of tension in the body and then suddenly releasing that through an orgasm. Rather than focusing on building pressure, sexual techniques from both China and India involve slowly and gently stimulating the body's erogenous zones in order to nourish the body with pleasurable flows of energy. Rather than building to a climax, it is all about learning to relax into gentler and gentler currents of bliss. For men, avoiding ejaculation is paramount: when you feel that orgasm might be imminent, you back off in order to allow the body to continue to relax into the pleasure.

Remember how in the previous section I introduced a practice that involved relaxing and relishing the pleasant sensations that arise, sinking deeply into those as if you're descending into a warm bath of sparkles? Well, the same thing very much applies here. And remember how I said that eventually the physical body dissipates, leaving just a vibrating and sparkling galaxy of bliss dancing in empty space? The same thing will happen here. The key is to keep relaxing into the field of sensations.

Do you remember how I said that you should feel self-conscious and embarrassed about the fact that you have a body that takes great pleasure in its own sensations? No you don't, because I never said that! If you're feeling that way, check and see if you have internalized repressive messages about sexuality from religious or cultural traditions that demonize this completely natural source of enjoyment and intimacy. It's also possible that you've been traumatized through previous sexual interactions and need some healing in this area before you can experience some of these subtleties. The very same

finger-widths below the navel deep in the core of the body. Other traditions refer to three dantian: the one just described, another at the heart, and a third in the middle of the skull. Like in Indian and Tibetan practices, the dantian are important locations for the visualization of deities and other spiritual symbols. In China such practices are often referred to as "inner alchemy," and these meditations are often metaphorically equated to the process of making an alchemical elixir within these locations of the body.

Another similarity between Indian, Tibetan, and Chinese systems is the idea of a circuit or pathway of energy along the midline of the body, connecting these energy centers. Various schools of Tantric Hinduism (most notably Shaiva forms) speak of a powerful source of energy that lies dormant in the area of the perineum. Personified as the snake-goddess Kundalini (literally, "the coiled one"), this energy can be awakened through specific yogic exercises and breathing techniques. Once awakened, the goddess rises up, winds through the energy pathways (*nadi*) that connect the chakras along the midline of the body, and eventually arrives in the crown. At this point, the practitioner experiences an expansion of consciousness, various types of spiritual wisdom, powers (*siddhis*), and other mystical experiences. A very similar process is explained in Vajrayana Buddhism, although they use different terminology. In the West, the term *Kundalini Yoga* is also a brand name for a type of energy-based yoga practice that is associated with the Sikh religion.

In Chinese practice, a somewhat analogous phenomenon is known as the "microcosmic orbit" or, more literally, the "small universe" (*xiaozhou*). Here, rather than rise up through the core of the body, the energy flows along the surface of the skin. Like Kundalini, the flow begins from the perineum and continues up the midline of the back of the body to the crown. Reaching the top of the head, however, it then continues down the forehead and down the midline of the front of the body back to the perineum, completing the circuit. In an adept practitioner of energywork, the microcosmic orbit flows unobstructed, bringing vitality, longevity, and spiritual transformation.

Phenomenology

So far, everything I've said in this section reflects how these components of the energy system are traditionally described in authoritative texts. These writings provide models to follow and can prepare practitioners for what to expect as the energy body opens up. From what I've seen in practice, however, most people who produce energetic openings with the methods we are discussing in this chapter experience a wider range of phenomena than strictly what is written in these texts.

Rather than a nice sequential opening of the chakras or dantians, most spiritual practitioners that I've talked with report feeling that various parts of the body open up at different times. For example, they experience the kind of free-flowing bliss I described in the previous sections of this chapter in their chest area before they feel it in their lower abdomen, or vice versa. They often feel like some parts of their energy system are easier to open while others remain stubbornly blocked.

Many spiritual practitioners also report experiencing surprising and unpredictable surges of energy in the body. These energetic anomalies may make your body feel like it's growing, shrinking, expanding, contracting, dissolving, or even disappearing altogether. These surges can also feel like they get stuck in certain places, creating weird sensations of pressure, itching, or pain. They sometimes can manifest as emotional, visual, auditory, or even psychic phenomena. You may suddenly start seeing lights, having out-of-body experiences, or traveling to astral planes or other ethereal worlds. They can also produce unexpected physical effects called *kriyas*, including spontaneous shivering, facial grimaces, utterances or sounds, movements of the limbs, contortions of the hands, and even whole-body postures. With time, as the whole energy system becomes more open, these sorts of phenomena gradually smooth out and eventually disappear.

Someone whose kundalini or microcosmic orbit is activated and unobstructed is likely to experience a tremendous amount of physical energy. They almost certainly will also feel that their spiritual practice is supercharged, that they are making much more rapid progress than they did when there were energetic blockages. These flows of energy regularly produce all kinds of mystical or awakening experiences. Someone with an open energy system like this has passed the point of no return, their entire being is now immersed in the process of enlightenment and is propelling them forward (whether they are ready or not!).

BOX 6.3: Getting Started with
Circulating Energy in the Body

Whereas other exercises in this chapter have helped you become aware of increasingly subtle sensations in the body, here we will take the first step toward circulating those energies through the body in an intentional way. Let's again start with the post stance exercise as presented in the "moving meditation" section (box 6.1). You'll want to follow all of the instructions presented there for a good five to ten minutes before proceeding.

Once you are steeped in the gentle buzz of your subtle body sensations in this static position, it is time to begin to circulate these energies through your body. So far, when you've done the post stance, you've left your arms at the side of your body, with your palms facing inward at each other. Now, we are going to move the arms in a way that draws energy up through your body.

Keeping your arms straight but relaxed, raise them up in front of you until they are vertically above your head. As you do this, inhale a deep belly breath. Make the movement synchronize with your breath, so that lifting your arms takes as long as your inhalation. When your arms are directly above your head, your palms will still be facing each other. Pause here at the apex of the movement for two or three seconds, retaining your breath. Gently stretch your fingers upward away from your body, elongating your spine from the tailbone to the crown.

Now exhale deeply from your belly while opening your arms out to the sides, slowly bringing them back to their original position. Again, synchronize your breath with this movement. When you are back in the original position, pause briefly and stretch your fingers toward the ground before inhaling again. Repeat.

(continues)

As you inhale raising your arms, sweep your awareness along the midline of your body from your feet to your crown. As you exhale while lowering your arms, sweep your awareness back along the midline from top to bottom. As your awareness passes through your body, take in any sensations that might be present. Don't get hung up on closely investigating any one particular location; just keep sweeping through the body in a fluid and gentle way. Eventually, it may feel like the sensations themselves are moving up and down your body. If that is the case, you may be able to just rest your attention on the body as a whole and allow these currents of sensation to flow up and down spontaneously.

Slowly repeat this exercise for five to ten minutes. When you are finished, the usual advice is to end on the downward motion, returning the energy back down through your legs and into the earth. Spend a moment or two relaxing in post stance to give your body a chance to ground. See if you perceive a difference in your emotions, attention, and physical energy levels as you go about the rest of your day.

BOX 6.4: A Variation: Circulating Light

There are many Asian traditions that use the metaphor or the visual image of light in order to help to direct energy. This is as common in many kinds of Hindu and Buddhist meditations as it is in Chinese energy practices. To give a variation on the preceding exercise that incorporates the visualization of light, repeat the exercise as before, with the following additions:

During the inhalation phase of the exercise, imagine or visualize that you are drawing a bright light up through your body. It can be of any color that strikes you as relaxing, sacred, or energizing (golden yellow, like a sunflower, works best for me). As you raise your arms, see this light streaming down from the heavens via your crown into your body and filling your body from your feet on upward as if you were an empty vessel. When your arms arrive at the apex straight above your head, imagine or visualize this light shining brightly and pervading your entire body. During the exhalation phase, imagine or visualize that the light now extrudes from your body, illuminating the space around you in all directions.

Over time, repetition of this visualization will improve your ability to actually "see" the light in your mind's eye.

DETOURS ON THE PATH

As I have noted in other chapters, the spiritual practices discussed throughout this book can occasionally lead to unexpected and undesired outcomes. One of the pitfalls that you should already be on the lookout for, since it came up in the last chapter, is the misuse of sexuality by spiritual teachers. We don't need to go over this topic again. I'll just say here that, in my view, any teacher who engages in sexual relations of any kind with any of their students is a fraud. Period. In general, I think it is all too easy for Tantric sexual practices to be misused in ways that are extremely harmful to individuals and communities of practitioners. Given these dangers, my own strong feeling is that these kinds of practices should only be done on one's own or within the context of a committed and loving relationship instead of with teachers or strangers in workshops.

Another issue that may arise in this kind of work is symptoms from energy blockages, already mentioned briefly in the last section. The exercises I introduced in this chapter are very gentle and basic, meaning they will be safe and effective for almost all people. Notwithstanding, every person has blockages hidden in their system, so it is unreasonable to expect that you will be able to completely avoid all difficulties when opening up your energy body.

If you experience strong side effects, this can be emotionally and physically challenging. Energetic symptoms can mimic or even cause physical or mental illnesses, and in the extreme, these can be debilitating. That being said, it has become fashionable in certain Western spiritual circles to blame every ailment or setback one experiences in life on "Kundalini syndrome" or "qigong deviation." If your difficulties are truly the result of kundalini or energy imbalances, then the most effective treatment will be grounding practices. (This is one reason why I think that grounding should be a central part of every spiritual explorer's daily regimen from the very beginning.)

If simple grounding is not enough, there are many other techniques to balance out the energy body taught in qigong, yoga, and other spiritual disciplines. Additionally, there are Asian healing arts such as such as acupuncture, Reiki, shiatsu, Thai massage, and many others that also work with energy. These modalities have medical rather than spiritual goals. However, they share the same worldview as the spiritual practices introduced here, so therapists grounded in these disciplines tend to understand energy imbalances and can in many cases go straight to the problem. Specialists of Ayurveda, Chinese herbs, Sowa Rigpa, and other Asian medical systems that address physical symptoms in natural ways can also be quite helpful.

If energy imbalances arise in your practice, you should always get yourself checked out by a physician in addition to whatever holistic care you are receiving. Get whatever scans or tests are needed in order to rule out any medical abnormalities. That being said, you might want to be careful about discussing too many of the details of your spiritual practice with medical professionals who don't have an understanding of Asian traditions or energetic medicine. I have heard stories about people who were experiencing energetic difficulties getting misdiagnosed by psychiatrists and being medicated or even committed to mental hospitals when it's likely all they needed was some intensive grounding.

If your unwanted symptoms are primarily of an emotional nature, therapy can be super helpful as well. One circumstance that traditional Asian spiritual teachings often neglect to talk much about is how spiritual practice can trigger difficult emotions and memories. While this is changing in the contemporary Western context, Asian religion and philosophy traditionally did not well understand the unconscious mind, shadow material, complex trauma, and other aspects of the psychological landscape. Fortunately, these realities are well-traversed territory for modern therapists, many of whom also have training in Asian spirituality. In fact, I think it is now routine for serious Western practitioners and teachers to integrate therapy into spiritual practice. The hope is that combining the best of both worlds leads to more rapid personal transformation, with more stable transitions and fewer side effects.

If you need help navigating these waters for yourself or to help a fellow explorer, consult the resources for spiritual emergency mentioned in box 3.6.

As was the case with the previous two chapters, the practices briefly introduced here are complex, ancient systems of practice with many divergent variations. There are many more advanced facets of energy that I have not been able to include here, such as energywork to "clear" spaces, heal illnesses, or tap into psychic powers. My intention here has been to provide a starting point from which you can embark upon further exploration and investigation if you are interested. As before, I've provided some resources below to help you on your way.

BOX 6.5: Additional Resources
for Exploring the Energy Body

PODCASTS

- *Buddha at the Gas Pump*—Interviews with spiritual teachers of all kinds. Keyword-search the past episodes to find teachers affiliated with different approaches mentioned in this chapter, and then listen to the interviews to sample their teachings on the integration of the body into Asian spirituality.

BOOKS

- Willa Blythe Baker, *The Wakeful Body: Somatic Mindfulness as a Path to Freedom*—Clear instructions for integrating the body into your meditation practice
- Nida Chenagtsang, *Karmamudra: The Yoga of Bliss*—Tibetan approaches to sacred sexuality, including healing from sexual trauma
- Christopher D. Wallis, *Tantra Illuminated: The Philosophy, History, and Practice of a Timeless Tradition*—A comprehensive overview of Shaiva Tantra
- Livia Kohn, *Health and Long Life: The Chinese Way*—A brief introduction to the whole range of "arts of qi" from Taoism and Chinese culture

There are, of course, many Asian spiritual practices related to body-centered practices that I have not mentioned here. Some of these have been omitted because they cross a line from spiritual exploration into religious indoctrination. Others have been omitted because they prioritize physical prowess or sexual endurance over spiritual development, and thus don't fit with the goals of this book. The resources I recommend contain additional information about other practices not covered here, and I encourage you to use discrimination in deciding what to further pursue.

CHAPTER 7

PUTTING IT ALL TOGETHER

While of course there are overlaps among them, the spiritual techniques outlined earlier in this book essentially fall into one of three categories: realizing the nondual nature of perception, opening the heart, or spiritually transforming the energy body. Ultimately, these three kinds of practice support, overlap, and interpenetrate one another. I personally would say that they are completely inseparable. However, different Asian traditions have valued and prioritized these categories differently.

Some groups or traditions emphasize a single area of cultivation over and above all the others. Practitioners of Hindu bhakti, for example, primarily practice devotion to certain deities and gurus. Pure Land Buddhists likewise primarily focus on opening the heart with prayer and surrender to Amitabha Buddha. Followers of Advaita and most schools of Zen Buddhism, on the other hand, place the vast majority of their focus on realizing the nondual nature of perception through intensive meditation or koan practice. Martial artists or Chinese medicine practitioners most often work exclusively with the energy body.

Other traditions embrace two of these categories of spiritual practice while largely overlooking the third. For example, Theravada Buddhism ranks meditation as primary while giving attention to opening the heart through practices like metta bhavana and devotion to the Buddha. Most forms of Mahayana Buddhism embrace nonduality and open-heartedness equally, calling the combination of wisdom and compassion the "two wheels" or "two wings" of the tradition. However, as discussed above, both of these forms of Buddhism have historically tended to neglect or even demonize the body. Meanwhile, the system laid out in Patañjali's *Yoga Sutras* goes into great detail about nondual perception and energetic cultivation but doesn't explicitly include any heart-opening practices.

The forms of Asian spiritual practice that most explicitly integrate all three areas are Taoism and the various forms of Tantra. But even here, exactly how these systems integrate them varies. In Tantric schools of Buddhism such as the Tibetan Vajrayana tradition, the three categories are usually introduced sequentially. When a practitioner first starts out, there is a lot of emphasis on devotional practices like guru yoga and deity yoga, as well as on practices intended to open your sense of compassion for all beings (in this tradition called *bodhicitta*). Once you have completed these so-called "preliminary practices"—which are all heart-opening techniques—you can then begin working on nondual realization through the practice of meditation. Eventually, once significant opening of your heart and perception have taken place, the energy body also comes to be integrated into your spiritual path through forms of yogic and breathing exercises. In contrast, Taoism begins with the body and devotional cultivation and later culminates with nondual practices. Finally, in Hindu forms of Tantra, such as Kashmiri Shaivism, it seems that it's the norm to cultivate all three of these categories simultaneously. In fact, I think some Tantric traditions would say that separating out these three modes of cultivation is creating false distinctions.

What about you? Where do you stand? Having read through the last three chapters, how do you rank the relative importance of nonduality, heart, and energy? Will you prioritize one, or two, or integrate all three?

I have noticed over time that certain trends in the way Western spiritual seekers answer these questions. There is actually some scholarly research that shows that Western women often tend to be energy whereas men often predominate in spaces that prioritize nonduality. Among my college students, I've noticed that humanities majors are more likely to relate to the heart and energy, whereas science majors generally relate more strongly to nonduality. I've also noticed among my friends and colleagues that people who are very intellectual often tend to exclusively prioritize nonduality—and sometimes have a hard time even understanding the importance of the other categories—while those who are more artistic often do the opposite.

Different strokes for different folks, of course, and please feel free to make the choice that works best for you. However, I personally think that the happiest, most spiritually balanced, and most well-adjusted people I have ever met—of all genders, majors, and personality types—are those who are making efforts to integrate all three kinds of spirituality. With this in mind, this chapter gives you some of my own thoughts on how to pull together the approaches introduced previously to create a sustainable and fulfilling spiritual practice that integrates your perception, heart, and body.

CHOOSE YOUR OWN ADVENTURE

In the contemporary period we are very lucky to have access to so much information about so many different spiritual paths. In earlier times, spiritual explorers were oftentimes limited, stuck only being able to learn whatever happened to be taught at the local temple up the road. Fortunately, thanks to the internet and global travel, we now have access to a huge range of methods and techniques. It's entirely possible to customize your own spiritual path in a way that is optimal for who you are, focuses on what you're interested in, and takes you where you want to go. My hope is that this book will give you the tools to be able to navigate the options and design your own spiritual path with confidence.

Also remember that there is nothing wrong with focusing exclusively on one particular tradition and fully devoting yourself to it. If at any point you find yourself in a nice camping spot, you can pitch your tent and hang out there. If the result of reading this book is that you realize you want to become a Buddhist, a Hindu, or whatever, then go for it!

However, I've chosen to write this particular book in a way that fits with my personal approach to spiritual development. I've always been motivated to move around and explore the territory. What spirituality has looked like for me has consequently changed over the years. The first five years, I was deeply into Theravada Buddhism. Then, I got into a twenty-year period where I pretty much only was interested in Mahayana. Then, out of the blue, approaches to nonduality from Dzogchen became more of a priority for me. All along, for nearly thirty years, I've maintained a daily practice of Hathayoga that I originally learned in a Hindu ashram. And I've consistently resonated with early Taoist philosophy.

Maybe you could say that I have had a generally Tantric approach, in that I equally focus on practices for transforming perception, heart, and energy. But if that's the case, then it's my own particular flavor of Tantra, because I have chosen the specific practices based on what resonates with me personally. (I also have embraced other spiritual practices that are not derived from Asia, but I'll leave those out since they're beyond the scope of the discussion in this book.) No one tradition had all the ingredients that clicked with me, so I pieced together the ideal combination that worked for my bodymind, life situation, and overall goals. This book is intended for people who are interested in a similar type of individual customization.

This kind of DIY spirituality is *not* anything goes—it must be founded on a solid base or the whole structure will be unsteady. Earlier, I recommended you begin by establishing yourself in the core practices outlined in chapter 3 before beginning any further exploration. This is both essential for your safety and also will expedite your progress once you start diving into more advanced practices. Once you have been established in the core practices for at least a few months, I'd then advise you to choose at least one technique from each of the preceding three chapters and put them together to form a daily practice that focuses on nonduality, heart, and energy in a balanced way. (I've provided a handy chart at the end of this section for your convenience.)

These are your building blocks, but I encourage you to use your own discretion in how you put the pieces together. Do you feel like giving a bit more time to your meditation practice than the others? Feel free. Do you feel like putting the energy practice first because you find this helps you to be less sleepy in your meditation? You're in charge.

When thinking about assembling your daily routine, you'll want to make sure that you're not setting your bar too high. Most people who start out trying to do hours and hours of practices each day will soon find their interest and willpower petering out. It's also important not to get super goal oriented or to allow spirituality to become one more thing on your to-do list that's stressing you out. If you find yourself slipping into this kind of achievement-driven mentality, take a break and go back to the basics introduced in chapter 3 for a while.

On the other hand, let's be honest. If you're only doing fifteen minutes of practice per day, you aren't really giving your system a high enough "dose" to really make any fundamental changes. In my experience, the sweet spot for serious spiritual practice is somewhere between one and two hours a day. However, as you start to make progress, you may find yourself effortlessly spending more and more of your day in practice. Eventually, you may find that it takes on a life of its own—like your practice is the main thing (or one of the main things) in your life, and you fit other things in around that.

Stay realistic about the pace of spiritual self-transformation. As I mentioned several times previously, think in terms of years instead of days. But if you're putting in an hour or more each day, you can anticipate seeing astounding signs of positive transformation after your first year of diligently practicing. If you do not, maybe change up what you're doing. Never lock yourself into something that's not working for you. If you've given a particular practice two or three months and it doesn't seem to be clicking, pick something different. Or perhaps you've been doing something for a while and it's been working, but you realize it's now starting to get stale. That's totally normal. When you do make a change, pick another practice from the same category as the one you are stopping so that you maintain a consistent balance between the three realms of nonduality, heart, and energy.

It is most likely that when you first start out you won't know what your spiritual orientation is, and you will have to explore a bit to find it. Maybe you get lucky and the first things you try will really rock your world. Much more likely, you'll change tacks a few different times. Maybe you'll try everything and decide that Asian spiritual traditions are not your thing after all. All of the above are okay. The point is you have to find out what works for you and then do your best to fully embody your own path.

Over the long term, most serious practitioners find that spiritual practice begins to open up one of the three areas first before gradually spreading to the others. The order in which this will happen for you seems to have more to do with how your own bodymind is wired than anything else. Do you remember my own story I told in chapter 1? When I first started out, I focused on vipassana and yoga (that is, perception and energy) for about five years. But then I discovered metta bhavana, and after only a few weeks of practice I experienced a dramatic heart opening that changed my life. For whatever reason, and unbeknownst to me, I was wired for my heart center to open up first. It was only many years later that equally dramatic perceptual and energetic openings took place for me.

I am one hundred percent sure that your journey will look different than mine. Perhaps you will taste nondual perception first, and your heart will open later. Maybe you will connect more with stilling the mind rather than the more active investigative and movement-based practices that have worked better for me. Most likely you will experience more gradual unfoldings rather than big mystical experiences like I've had. Or perhaps it will take you decades to open up your energy, but then one day your kundalini will suddenly awaken and you will blast through the rest of the transformation process in lightning speed. Your own journey may be completely unique, different than anyone else you've ever heard of. You simply cannot know in advance how you are configured or how your path will unfold. Therefore, in my opinion, the best thing to do is to just keep working on all three categories of practice simultaneously and to allow things to proceed naturally however they will.

However your spiritual journey unfolds, comparing notes with other travelers can be useful. This is particularly true for those of us who are exploring the territory without belonging to a specific tradition. It sometimes can be helpful to check out discussion groups, online forums, and other places where Western spiritual seekers gather. But be aware that there is not a lot of support for the kind of exploration and customization I am advocating in this book. From what I've seen, online groups and social media accounts tend to focus on memes and platitudes that sound nice but are not really offering any solid or knowledgeable advice. Then there's the other end of the spectrum: groups dedicated to examining the details of one particular system, approach, or model of practice. Many such groups have strong viewpoints about departing from their established tradition, and if you even mention customizing your spiritual path in a setting like that, you can quickly find yourself ostracized.

In contrast to this hard-core stance, if you ask me, I think it's obvious that there's more than one way for human beings to grow and flourish. My firm conviction is that there are wonderful tools and perspectives offered by all of the world's spiritual traditions, which can be helpful for different people at different times of their lives. The important point is to really learn to appreciate the differences among these practices so you can find what resonates with you personally and then go do that with confidence.

Imagine, for comparison, if this book you're holding in your hands was about exploring the arts instead of exploring spirituality. If there was a chapter in which I discussed various styles of dance, one on painting, one on music, one on film, and so forth. Who could argue that one of those fields is "more artistic" than the others? Such questions are nonsensical because they are demanding that we pit high-level achievements in completely different arenas against one another. Instead, why not take it all in, appreciating and celebrating the amazing range of art that human beings can produce?

I'd make the same argument for spirituality. Someone like Ramana Maharshi was truly a virtuoso of pure consciousness, while Thich Naht Hanh was just as clearly a maestro of emptiness. Ama is just as much a paragon of open-heartedness as Geeta Iyengar was of the refinement of yogic postures. The fact that people can reach such heights in different areas of spirituality, to me, is clear confirmation that there's no one-size-fits-all path for anyone. I think rating their achievements against one another is nonsensical. Like the arts, spirituality is a wondrous and fascinating dimension of human experience that should be explored, celebrated, and enjoyed in all of its rich diversity.

What about ordinary people like you and me? We may not have as much raw talent as the virtuosos I just mentioned, but some of us will, by our nature, be drawn to appreciate certain forms of spirituality over others. We might find ourselves more drawn to questions about how consciousness and perception work, or to how we can create more love and intimacy in the world, or to how we can meld more completely into the energetic flow of life. In the same way, some people will resonate with Advaita and find that it really works for them, while others will respond more to Zen, yoga, qigong, or whatever. We will find that we have more talent and joy learning certain techniques over others.

Why are there these differences? Well, why are some people drawn to painting and others more to film? Why do some kids pick up the piano quickly and love it, while others labor over practicing and quit as soon as they are allowed to? If you asked the Asian traditions, they'd say such differences are due to people's individual karma. As usual, I'm agnostic on questions of what's ultimately going on, but it's clear that these differences exist. Given that fact, does it make any sense to debate which spiritual system is the single best one for all to follow? Why not focus instead on discovering where our own spiritual talents and inclinations lie, and then work to fully bring those innate gifts to fruition? Instead of conforming to someone else's ideals or trying to convince people to conform to ours, why don't we each discover for ourselves where our own path lies?

BOX 7.1: Table of Practices Introduced in This Book

In chapter 3, I introduced a handful of core practices, while chapters 4–6 further outlined the three different areas of nondual perception, heart opening, and working with energy. Optimally, you can develop a blend of practices that provides balance among all of these forms of spiritual cultivation. It's kind of like how athletes who cross-train are generally more balanced, skilled, and all-around fit than those who intensely train in only one thing. My hope is that presenting this information all together here can inspire you to become a cross-trained spiritual explorer with skills in multiple realms. I suggest doing all the practices from chapter 3 and then at least one in each column from chapters 4–6.

CORE PRACTICES (CH. 3)		
MINDFULNESS		
• Grounding Practice 1: Corpse Pose Belly Breathing (Shavasana)		
• Grounding Practice 2: Post Stance (Zhanzhuang)		
• Taking Care		
• Letting Go		
PERCEPTION (CH. 4)	**HEART (CH. 5)**	**ENERGY (CH. 6)**
• Self-Inquiry	• Metta Bhavana	• Moving Meditation
• Vipassana	• Tonglen	• Meditation on
• Mantra Practice	• Spirit Offerings	Erotic Bliss
• Doing-Nothing Meditation	• Surrender Ritual	• Circulating Energy
		• Circulating Light

TO THINE OWN SELF BE TRUE

In addition to each of us connecting or resonating with different techniques, we also each have different ways that we can most naturally integrate spirituality into our daily lives. There's another metaphor I often use to describe this, that of an ecosystem. Take the Serengeti, for example. Isn't it fascinating how each of the inhabitants is perfectly adapted to their own discrete niche? We wouldn't come along and criticize hippos for wallowing in the mud or giraffes for having necks that are too long, would we? We wouldn't ask lions why they aren't acting like rhinos or expect hyenas to behave like cheetahs, would we? Of course not. On the contrary, we appreciate the biodiversity. We marvel at the ingenuity behind the evolutionary processes that developed so many unique creatures to fill each particular niche in the environment.

I'm suggesting that we can take the same approach to the diversity of ways that people can live out a spiritual life. For example, there are some people who are clearly more adapted to living as monastics. Such individuals are usually a bit introverted, thrive on being apart from the world, and enjoy long bouts of solitude and silence. For whatever reason, they are designed in such a way that they're a good fit for that particular niche. (Again, some would say it's karma.) But does that mean that that's the only way to be spiritual? No! There are countless other people who are more well-adapted to living a spiritual life right in the thick of society. These individuals might have more extroverted qualities. They enjoy being part of the world, not apart from it. And that's perfectly okay.

Within the Asian traditions, there are certain teachings, ideals, and lifestyles that were historically more geared toward monastics and others that were developed with laypeople in mind. In other words, some systems of Asian spirituality are designed for hippos and others for giraffes.

If you ask me, the most meaningful spirituality is the one that's authentically integrated into the life that you yourself are living. If you are a person who is in a loving partnership and raising children, for example, instead of feeling like you need to abandon all that and go live in a monastery in order to be spiritual, why not simply make your relationships a fruitful field for exploring heart-opening practices? If you are engaged in a fulfilling job where you find that you can help other people or bring them joy, then why can't your work become your karma yoga dedicated to benefiting all beings? If you enjoy creative pursuits such as writing, making music, or gardening, then why can't these become the arena for you to dance with the creative energies of the divine? If you are naturally a more physical person, then why not use your innate abilities in this area to connect with the energy body? If you are naturally more sensual, then why not use that to connect with the vibrant power of Shakti? If you are naturally kind, then why not use that to connect with universal metta? The possibilities are endless—just let your spirituality be true to your own nature.

In my opinion, it's less about *changing* who you are than *discovering* who you are. Because spirituality is about realizing and embodying our own deepest being, our best advisor for how to integrate it into our lives is not going to be online forums, courses, books, or even enlightened teachers. Our truest, most accurate guide is always going to be our own inner guidance.

The Buddha referred to being "a lamp unto yourself." Other traditions talk about your inner guru, your guardian spirit, your power of discernment, or simply your intuition. Whatever you choose to call it, this inner guidance has nothing to do with your mind or your thoughts. (It's quite easy to *think* that a particular spiritual path is a good fit for you, even while your inner guidance is telling you something quite different.) Nor is it about your emotions. (We all know that constantly giving our emotions what they seem to want or need at any given moment can be counterproductive for our overall health and growth.)

If your inner guidance is not located in your intellect or emotions, then where do you find it? For me, my inner guidance manifests in my body as a subtle sense of contentment, clarity, coherence, and connection. Over time, I've learned to check in and trust this feeling. Whenever I'm in doubt about something, whether it's something related to spirituality, a big decision about life more generally, or anything really, I tune in to my body to see if I can find that sense. When I feel that way, I take it as an indication that I'm on the right track. If I find instead that I feel out of alignment or feel any kind of unsettledness, unease, or disconnection—or even if I just feel a bit blank inside—then I know that my inner guidance is not aligned with this decision.

Some of the best tools I know to help you find, refine, and calibrate your own inner guidance are the grounding practices I introduced in chapter 3. It's only when your body is aligned and grounded, and your mind is calm, that you can clearly sense your inner guidance.

If you ask me, this is the only compass you need on the journey of spiritual exploration. If your spiritual practice is well aligned with your inner guidance, then over time you will find that spirituality begins to spread to more and more aspects of your life. It's as if every dimension of your life is spontaneously reorganized and put into service of your growth.

Along the way, you probably will hear your inner guidance telling you that certain aspects of your life—particular activities, or relationships, or habits, say—no longer serve you and that you have to let them go. Sometimes that letting go can be difficult, accompanied by much sorrow, conflict, or fear. When going through a rough patch like this, keep listening for and trusting your inner guidance. The mindfulness, grounding, and other techniques discussed in chapter 3—and perhaps particularly those in the "Letting Go and Finding Flow" section—can be super helpful in keeping you on track.

If you are honest with yourself and diligent about following your inner guidance, over time, intensive spiritual practice can and probably will seriously rock your boat or even completely capsize the life you've been accustomed to. You might one day even realize that you've been fooling yourself for decades about some pretty fundamental things. Like a zebra that has been telling itself it's a lion, you might come to realize you have been living a life that's not your own. You might find you need to give up a carefully cultivated career, move across the country or even abroad, end a marriage, or perhaps, yes, even renounce the householder life and become a monastic. When such moments come, people around you may think you've gone mad—and you may even find that part of you agrees with them. Before making a major life-disrupting decision, it may also be a good idea to sit with it for six months or a year, so as to be completely sure that this is the direction in which you are being called. Ultimately, though, if you are sure you are acting in accord with your inner guidance (and not your thoughts or emotions), then you can trust that you are heading in the right direction.

When a major reorientation or rebalancing process like this takes place in your life, it can be supremely difficult in the moment. However, following the path indicated by your inner guidance will inevitably be worth it in the end. Just imagine the relief the zebra will feel when it finally throws off that silly fake lion's mane it's been wearing, stops lurking behind the shrubbery, and embodies its long-repressed natural instincts to gallop across the open grasslands. Your inner guidance wants for you to be your authentic self, fully and unapologetically, whatever that is.

CARRY YOUR OWN BAGGAGE

You might have gathered from the discussion in this book that an authentic spiritual path is not always a gilded path of bliss and happiness. As we saw in chapter 3, "spiritual materialism" that is all about feeling good, looking good, and being trendy is a near enemy to authentic spirituality. In contrast, every single person I've ever met who has had an authentic spiritual opening has agreed that it is hard work and there were parts of the path that were extremely difficult to navigate.

Many new spiritual seekers are taken by surprise by how nonlinear the process of spiritual opening is. Authentic spiritual unfolding is often kicked off by a powerfully transformative experience of some kind. Frequently, this initial experience is so eye-opening that people assume they have spontaneously become enlightened and their work is done. Nothing could be further from the truth. As the old adage says, "What goes up must also come down," and soon enough every spiritual high is followed by a rough patch of integration and growth.

Your own path may feel like a bumpy road or maybe an out-of-control roller coaster. Tremendous clarity may open up, followed by periods when everything seems to be frustratingly obscure. You may oscillate back and forth for months or years between extremes of bliss, joy, and clarity on the one hand, and despair, darkness, terror, and confusion on the other. At times you may lose touch with your inner guidance or even experience a "dark night of the soul." While most Asian spiritual traditions don't go into much detail about the difficulties of the path, one traditional model that does is the "stages of insight" from Theravada Buddhism. This model explicitly includes fear, misery, disgust, and other negative experiences as landmarks on the path. At least they're being honest about the range of experiences you can expect. (I've actually met people who have a form of PTSD that was caused by the intensity of their spiritual experiences.)

In any case, this process of two steps forward, one step back is actually a sign of a true spiritual opening. If your path is all smooth and blissful, that's a pretty good sign that you're likely deluding yourself and not actually having an authentic experience. The brighter the light of spirituality is shining in your life and the more you are learning to embody your true authentic self, the more all the parts of you that you have previously tucked away in the shadows will want to come forth into the light. Exactly how this happens for you will vary according to your own particular makeup. It could come in the form of overwhelming emotions, energy blockages, or physical symptoms, or like the Buddha you might even face down a literal or metaphorical horde of demons coming to assail you. One way or another, be prepared for all of your traumas, repressed memories, and other "karmic imprints" (in Sanskrit called *samskaras*) to resurface. When this happens, you will be terrified, or horrified, or both. You will be tempted to stuff that all back into the darkness, to gloss over it quickly and tell yourself you've successfully dealt with it, or to simply ignore it all. Giving in to that kind of impulse is often called "spiritual bypassing."

Let me tell a story to illustrate. On one of my trips to southern China back in the late 1990s, I visited a sacred Buddhist mountain named Emeishan. I woke up early, before sunrise, to traverse the long and winding path up to the temple at the summit. I spent the whole day climbing literally tens of thousands of stairs. At last, just before sunset, with legs exhausted, I arrived at the summit prepared to take in the incredible vista. I had seen the view in photos before: temple buildings surrounded by misty mountains, just like a classical brush painting from Chinese history. I couldn't wait.

Imagine how surprised I was to find the top of the mountain crowded with people jostling to get photos of the view. I had seen hardly anyone on the climb up. Where did they all come from?

It was only then that I noticed there was a bus stop on the back side of the mountain. Instead of climbing the long trail of stairs, these people had taken the shortcut of driving up! However, the buses couldn't get to the very top, so the passengers still had a climb of several hundred yards to get from the bus stop to the summit. Some people actually climbed that last portion, but many chose to be carried on sedan chairs the rest of the way. They comfortably rested their heads on fluffy pillows while porters hauled them up the staircase. (Mind you, this was not because they had any difficulty walking—it was simply because they were too lazy to do so.)

To me, this is a perfect metaphor for spiritual bypass. A spiritual bypasser wants the glorious vistas from the top of the sacred mountain but wants to avoid the hard work of actually having to get there. True spirituality, in contrast, is often humbling and sometimes even humiliating. It's often disorienting and lonely, and you may occasionally feel like you are losing your mind. It's scary, and sometimes you may even fear for your life. A spiritual bypasser wants to skip over all that stuff and just get to the bliss.

Unfortunately, thinking that you can skip over all of the hard work is a deep misunderstanding about what the spiritual journey is actually about. If the goal was just to have bliss or altered states of consciousness, then that would be easy. But if the goal is to fundamentally shift the baseline of how you experience your self, your life, and everything else in a permanent and ongoing way, there simply is no shortcut. You can't just take a pill or use an app to get to that kind of thoroughgoing realization instantaneously. I know it sounds clichéd, but it is actually the arduous journey itself that produces the transformation. Ten thousand bus rides will never get you what you'll get from climbing ten thousand steps on your own just once.

I'm not telling you anything you don't already know. There is literally no kind of human endeavor where you can just skip right to the end and be amazing at it. It's always the hard work itself that produces the excellence. You can't just decide to be a pro golfer and never work on your swing, because it's working on the swing that makes you good at golf. You can't just declare yourself a concert pianist and never practice your scales, because it's the ability to play the scales that makes you a pianist. Just so, you can't magically become enlightened without putting in the blood, sweat, and tears that go into actually walking the spiritual path from beginning to end.

Unlike on Emeishan, on an authentic spiritual path, not only is there no bus up the back but there are also no porters. You not only have to climb every step yourself; you also have to carry your own baggage. All of it. Contrary to popular myth, just because you had some spiritual experiences, it doesn't mean you've got your act together in other aspects of your life. It doesn't mean that you are great at interpersonal relationships. It doesn't mean you've worked through your past traumas or other psychological issues. If anything, it will show you just how much work you have to do untangling all of your mess. Whatever you've stuffed away in the shadows that you don't want to deal with, whatever you've been repressing, whatever you've been lying to yourself about—all of the baggage you're bringing on this trip must eventually be unpacked, faced, worked through, accepted, and integrated.

Asian traditions offer some insights that can be helpful in working with your baggage. For example, the basic practices I introduced in chapter 3 will go a long way toward helping to lighten your load. When you find yourself in trouble, you can fall back on these basics. However, at some point or another, you are likely to also need something more. It is at this point that an experienced spiritual teacher or guide might be extremely helpful, even indispensable.

Connecting with your inner guidance is especially important at this juncture, and a good teacher or a healthy spiritual group should always be empowering you to do so. Listen carefully to your own inner guidance to ensure that these relationships are helpful, that your boundaries are being respected, and that it's a good fit for you. It is precisely at this point that you are at your most vulnerable, so reflect carefully and choose wisely. The vibe should feel more like you are communing with spiritual friends on an equal basis rather than entering into a situation where people have power over you.

On my own journey, I periodically have reached out to a variety of teachers, coaches, and therapists to check in and gain a little perspective with a particular challenge or issue. Because I don't affiliate with any particular tradition and haven't been part of any particular group, it means I have had no qualms about reaching out to all sorts of people who I feel might be beneficial to talk with.

Through this process, I have gained a lot of insights into the range of tools that Asian spiritual traditions can offer. On the other hand, I also have come to realize that there's a lot that Asian spiritual traditions are not particularly good at addressing. For example, they historically have never had much to say about how to integrate deep spiritual or mystical experiences into daily life issues like raising kids and going to work. Since they focus on transcending the self, they don't tend to have any advice for healthy ego development. They don't have much to offer for dealing with major trauma, PTSD, or mental health issues either.

Fortunately, there are a lot of specific tools outside Asian traditions that can be really helpful for navigating such difficult terrain. For example, engaging in therapy that is based on Western models of psychology is something a lot of spiritual explorers find immensely valuable. Speaking personally, I have in the past gained a lot of extremely helpful perspectives from Jungian psychology, integral philosophy, Feldenkrais, and neo-shamanism, among other things. But that's just what resonated for me. You might find other things to be more helpful to you in dealing with your own baggage.

These tools do not always have clear corollaries in ancient Asian philosophical or religious thought, but nevertheless I think they can often be practiced alongside Asian spirituality in ways that lead to a faster and less troublesome integration process with less likelihood of spiritual bypass. Because these Western techniques are beyond the scope of this book, I won't go into them any further here. However, I'll recommend one or two books at the end of the chapter that can be useful starting points.

ARRIVING AT THE GOAL

At long last, let's come back to a question we asked back at the very beginning of this book: Where is this journey of spiritual exploration headed? And, come to think of it, how will we know when we've arrived at that goal?

At this point in the book, you can perhaps better appreciate why I insisted in chapter 1 that divergent traditions subscribe to different versions of enlightenment. It turns out that each tradition's understanding of enlightenment depends on which practices it prioritizes. In most forms of Hinduism, for example, fully stabilizing one's mind in pure consciousness represents the pinnacle of human experience. One measure that is frequently held up as a litmus test of enlightenment in Hindu circles is whether you maintain pure conscious awareness at all times, including while dreaming and in deep sleep. Abiding in pure consciousness 24-7 in this way is referred to as *turiya* (meaning "the fourth state" after waking, dreaming, and deep sleep). The stabilization of turiya ultimately results in "liberation" (*moksha*), and the person who does so is said to be "liberated while still living" (*jivanmukta*).

The Theravada Buddhist definition of enlightenment also hinges on perception. But rather than aiming for pure consciousness, the goal is the complete cessation of consciousness. As discussed in chapter 4, cessation is a product of the practice of deep meditative absorption. In this tradition, there is no enlightenment without cessation. The first time cessation happens to someone, they are referred to as a "stream-enterer" (*sotapanna*). After repeated occurrences, they move through three additional stages until eventually gaining the status of a "worthy" (*arahant*). In this tradition, the latter is considered a fully enlightened person who has completed the karmic cycle of rebirths and will upon death finally be released from all future forms of existence.

In contrast, Mahayana Buddhism does not prioritize cessation at all. The goal instead is the realization of the emptiness or non-self nature of all phenomena accompanied by the full opening of the heart. One who has begun the process of opening both perception and the heart is referred to as a bodhisattva, and when they have completely perfected both, they are considered to be a buddha in their own right. For Mahayanists, the attainment of Theravada arahantship without the accompanying heart opening is called an "inferior vehicle" (*hinayana*).

Meanwhile, Vajrayana Buddhists, Shaivites, and other Tantrikas have even more lofty goals: nothing less than the full opening of nondual perception, the heart, and the energy body are the minimum criteria for enlightenment in these traditions. In many Tantric traditions, the body of a fully enlightened person should upon death burst into light or manifest a rainbow. When someone attains a "rainbow body," it is confirmation that the deceased has accomplished full perfection. A similar phenomenon is also usually required to confirm that a Taoist practitioner has become an immortal.

While they differ on the specific criteria for enlightenment, the Asian traditions agree that what is important is the shift in overall perspective or orientation rather than the specific steps that bring about the change. Along the way, you might experience pure consciousness, divine love, the dissolving of your body into energy, or any other kind of mystical happenings, but no matter how wonderful, none of these experiences are enlightenment in and of themselves. If it's a state that comes and goes or that you have to maintain with any kind of effort whatsoever, that simply cannot be enlightenment.

The Asian traditions also all share the conviction that enlightenment is not synonymous with the acquisition of any kind of powers or abilities. Many traditions talk about people developing special capacities (in Sanskrit called *siddhis*) as a side effect of the practice of spiritual methods. These include the ability to sense energies, see spirits or gods, travel to other realms, know other people's thoughts, or any number of other mysterious and wondrous gifts that result from practices of various kinds. If this happens to you, be sure to use these powers for good, and never for personal gain—but don't mistake any of them for enlightenment either. As we discussed in chapter 3, chasing after any kinds of experiences or powers is the very definition of spiritual materialism.

As opposed to all of those temporary things, the forms of Asian spirituality we have discussed in this book all define enlightenment as the permanent shift in the baseline of how you experience reality, not just while in meditation or in an altered state of consciousness but on a day-to-day, 24-7 basis. It's not an alternate reality—it's this exact same ordinary reality you are experiencing right this moment, with all its ups and downs, highs and lows—just seen in a different way. Seen in a nondual way in which your notion of being a self doesn't obscure your view. Seen with an open heart. Seen simultaneously as empty and as an interconnected manifestation of the divine energies of the cosmos. Seen as perfect just the way it is.

Some traditions (such as Zen, Dzogchen, and some forms of neo-Advaita) even go so far as to say that being enlightened is finally seeing with clarity that there's no such thing as enlightenment and that there never was any need to pursue it in the first place. To be sure, these traditions are not saying that we should just have ignored spiritual activity to drink beer in front of the TV. In fact, many of these very same traditions encourage you to passionately throw yourself into spiritual practice. It's just that, unlike the kind of spirituality that emphasizes striving and effort, these traditions are saying that we can relax our way into enlightenment. It's a goalless goal that we arrive at only once we stop seeking it.

So, will we ever arrive at the destination of being totally enlightened, totally perfected? If you ask me, perfect, full enlightenment is an ideal that is never actually attained. We are all aware of people like the Dalai Lama, Ramana Maharshi, Anandamayi Mai, and both of the Krishnamurtis (U.G. and Jiddu), who are held up as paragons of spiritual virtue. In reality, though, I think that these people would be the first to say that they themselves are works in progress.

While each Asian tradition might identify different stopping points along the path as the goal, to me the road to perfection seems endless. Let's say for argument's sake that you attain the level of enlightenment of one of those people I just mentioned. Even so, would there be no more work to be done in your life? No matter how wise you are, there's always more learning about how to express your personal wisdom and unique gifts for the world in more and more constructive ways. Won't you always be learning how to better help your community, how to be kinder and more gentle with others, how to be more sensitive to and intimate with wider and wider circles of beings? Won't there always be infinite opportunities to integrate spiritual perspectives further and further into your work life, family life, friendships, and other relationships? Won't there always be endless work to do integrating spiritual perspectives into politics, education, social justice, climate activism, and all kinds of social and cultural concerns? To quote the spiritual teacher and philosopher Ken Wilber, is it enough for you to "wake up," or do you also want to "grow up," "clean up," and "show up"? That means enlightenment is not just about becoming spiritually awakened but also becoming psychologically, ethically, and socially awakened as well.

Given the infinitely ongoing possibilities for integration across all of these dimensions of life, it makes no sense to me to draw an arbitrary line in the sand and say, "I have arrived at the final goal." But enough about my opinions. If you're going to forge your own spiritual path, and if you're going to walk it for yourself, then you can't adopt anyone else's definition of what the final goal looks like. As the architect of your own spiritual journey and porter of your own baggage, you'll also have to be the one who determines what kind of goal you are pursuing.

So, what do *you* think? What's *your* definition of enlightenment? When will *you* be satisfied that no further walking is necessary? On your own spiritual journey, is there a concrete goal to attain? Or is there just an endless forest of more paths to explore, more scenery to appreciate, and more experiences to learn from? You decide.

BOX 7.2: Resources Related to This Chapter

PODCASTS

- *Buddha at the Gas Pump*—Interviews with spiritual teachers of all kinds. A lot of the conversation in recent years on this podcast has concerned issues of integration discussed in this chapter (also frequently referred to as "embodiment"), and that topic is explored from a variety of perspectives.

BOOKS

- Ken Bradford, *The Psychology and Yoga of Liberation*—Integrating perspectives from Dzogchen with Western psychology
- Pema Chödrön, *When Things Fall Apart: Heart Advice for Difficult Times*—Practicing spirituality through life's difficulties
- John J. Prendergast, *In Touch: How to Tune In to the Inner Guidance of Your Body and Trust Yourself*—About discovering your inner guidance
- Joan Tollifson, *Death: The End of Self-Improvement*—Integrating spirituality in the face of illness and death
- Ken Wilber, *Integral Life Practice: A 21st-Century Blueprint for Physical Health, Emotional Balance, Mental Clarity, and Spiritual Awakening*—A theory of human development and a guide to integrating spirituality into different levels or stages of maturity

CHAPTER 8

THINKING CRITICALLY
ABOUT ASIAN SPIRITUALITY

So far in this book, I've introduced the history of Asian spiritual traditions, I've described the basic practices, and I've given you some of my thoughts both about how to integrate these practices together and where all of this can lead you. We've come a long way since we set out on this journey, but there are still a few things that I think are crucial to discuss before you set off into the wilderness on your own. In this final chapter, I'm going to share some important tools that I think can help you navigate the terrain in the future as you continue to read and learn about the traditions that have been introduced in this book.

You'll notice that in this chapter, I am changing my hats again, taking off the hat of the practitioner and putting back on that of the scholar. We college professors who teach religious studies love to talk about the importance of "critical thinking." In fact, we think this is one of the most important skills that we can teach our students. Thinking critically is not the same as criticizing. The latter just means raising objections or airing your negative opinions about a topic. Critical thinking, on the other hand, means developing an informed evaluation or opinion about it. It is the opposite of blindly accepting a story or an idea that's handed to you. Rather than just accepting what other people say, it's rolling up your sleeves and asking penetrating questions about the topic to reflect on it and understand it from a variety of different perspectives.

Sometimes people who are fundamentalist followers of a certain ideology feel that you should accept their ideas with no questions asked, and that by thinking critically you are undermining their faith or beliefs. However, my feeling is that thinking critically about something is actually the highest compliment. It means you care about the quality of the information you are receiving. It means you're taking a matter seriously enough to consider it thoroughly and analyze it from as many angles as you can.

Since we care deeply about the Asian spiritual traditions introduced throughout this book, let's pay them the compliment of doing some critical thinking about them together, shall we? Of course we won't be able raise every single critical perspective about these traditions in this one chapter, but we can definitely cover some ground. Here, I will concentrate on what I think are some important critical perspectives for you to bear in mind as you finish this book and move forward with your exploration of Asian traditions on your own.

ASIAN SPIRITUAL TRADITIONS ARE NOT PERFECT

Where do we start our process of thinking critically? My feeling is that one of the best starting points is simply to realize that Asian spiritual traditions are not perfect. Even if they have been around for thousands of years, even if many people say they are based on divine revelation, even if they have been endorsed by millions of people throughout history, even if they often lead to amazing personal transformation, it still doesn't mean that any of these traditions are always infallibly right or good or beneficial for everybody.

I've talked about how any given tradition might not be a good fit for your own values, needs, or goals. I've also discussed at length the many pitfalls and potential dark sides of these practices from an experiential perspective. But aside from all of that, I think it's also clear that many traditional Asian ideas or practices are actually hopelessly outdated or even downright objectionable in light of modern sensibilities. For example, I think that most people living in modern democratic societies would recoil from Hinduism's traditional teachings on caste. For literally thousands of years, this ingrained belief system divided the Hindu population into hierarchical social classes that determined what occupations people could hold, who they could marry, and how much respect they had in society based on which caste they happened to be born into. Today, although illegal in India, caste discrimination still is all too often used to disempower people, somewhat analogously to how people of color experience racial discrimination in the West. Lower-caste people, especially Dalits, the so-called "untouchable" caste that historically occupied the bottom of the caste hierarchy, continue to experience prejudice and structural barriers in their communities in India and even in diasporic communities around the world.

We could also rightly critique the instances of blatant misogyny that are found in traditional Asian religions. For example, did you notice how few women I mentioned when naming famous spiritual gurus or personalities in history? Many forms of Buddhism have considered it impossible for a woman to become enlightened, and women have not even been allowed to ordain as monastics in much of the Buddhist world. Women have not fared much better in other Asian spiritual traditions, although the Taoist tradition of "female alchemy" or *nüdan* is a notable exception.

The misogyny of these traditions is not just a matter of representation. This is a fundamental flaw that places limits on the efficacy of Asian spirituality. Because these traditions and practices are nearly always framed in a male-centric way, they often do not speak to the lived realities of female or gender-nonconforming practitioners. And many questions are left unanswered. For example, do energy practices designed for men work as well for people of other genders? Are there specific kinds of spiritual cultivation that can or should be done during menstruation or during pregnancy? Most Asian spiritual traditions have historically been silent on these matters because the audience they were addressing was almost exclusively male.

In addition to its gender problem, Asian spirituality is often a bastion of other kinds of biases and prejudices. Historical scriptures from around Asia often interpret physical and mental disabilities as karmic punishments for evil deeds done in previous lives. They often denigrate LGBTQ+ people and demonize non-heteronormative sexualities. Biases like these are not just historical artifacts but can be seen operating in modern times. Spiritual communities are also not necessarily racially diverse. In most parts of the West today, groups of practitioners often are either almost exclusively Asian or almost exclusively white. Not only do these so-called "parallel congregations" rarely intermix but neither represent particularly welcoming spaces for Latinos, African Americans, and people of other races and ethnicities. These kinds of dynamics have the effect of limiting the accessibility of Asian spirituality to wider groups of people.

Even when Asian spiritual teachings are not objectionable in themselves, all sorts of Asian spiritual concepts have historically been manipulated for nefarious purposes. I can think of plenty of examples where people have used the very ideas we've been talking about in this book to do tremendous harm. In my book *Buddhish*, for example, I talk about the use of Buddhist doctrines to justify kamikaze suicide missions by Japanese pilots during World War II, the assassination of seventy-seven innocent people by a Norwegian terrorist in 2011, and the ongoing genocide of the Rohingya ethnic group in Myanmar today.

Of course, it's not just Buddhism that has been manipulated in such ways. All the major religious belief systems have been used to justify unethical actions. Part of the reason such events can take place is the common assumption among adherents across Asian traditions that enlightened gurus or masters are perfect in every way and that we should have unquestioning faith in their teachings. This attitude means that it can sometimes be easy for rogue spiritual teachers to amass a whole army of brainwashed followers.

Unquestioning faith in gurus can result in a slippery slope toward millenarianism. This is a scholarly term for when a group identifies a particular individual as a messiah-like "chosen one" and claims that this teacher has been born on earth to bring forth the group's envisioned utopia. Millenarian thinking has historically led certain groups to become violent radicalized cults, not only in the West with groups like the Branch Davidians and Heaven's Gate but also in Asia. For example, numerous Taoist groups throughout Chinese history have embraced this kind of ideology, following their spiritual leader into rebellion against the government. In fact, the largest civil war in world history was the Taiping Revolution in mid-nineteenth-century China, a massive catastrophe instigated by a spiritual leader with millenarian ideas combining Christianity and traditional Chinese religious beliefs.

More recently, in 1984, followers of the Hindu guru Rajneesh poisoned 751 people in Oregon in the largest act of bioterrorism on American soil to date. The purpose of the poisoning was to influence local elections in favor of Rajneesh's ashram community. (These events are summarized in the documentary Netflix series *Wild Wild Country*.) Likewise, members of the Japanese religious cult Aum Shinrikyo released sarin gas in the Tokyo subway in 1995, killing 13 people. This group was inspired by millenarian interpretations of Buddhist and Hindu ideas.

Today, in the West, Asian spirituality continues to be mixed up with QAnon, white nationalism, and conspiracy theories of all kinds. (There's even a podcast called *Conspirituality* that is dedicated to exposing these connections.) And you should be aware that some of the largest international organizations promoting Asian spiritual traditions globally have covert political agendas. These are not always clearly announced publicly and sometimes are even actively obscured from prospective members.

Are you bristling at my suggestion that Asian spirituality may be flawed and politicized in these ways? If so, remember that critical thinking is about learning to be open-minded enough to consider things from all angles. I'm obviously not saying these traditions are all bad. No need to throw the baby out with the bathwater. But we can't hold forth an overly romanticized viewpoint that sees them as infallibly good either. The point is to remember that Asian spiritual traditions, like all human knowledge systems, are imperfect. They can be just as wrapped up in politics, war, social inequalities, and other social dynamics as the next. And they can just as readily be misused, corrupted, politicized, and weaponized.

Acknowledging all of this is essential to being able to navigate the contemporary spiritual landscape skillfully. So, take off the rose-colored glasses and put on your critical thinking cap when you are exploring this terrain. At the very least, always be sure to do your research before you join any spiritual organization, to make sure that you understand and support everything that they stand for.

ASIAN TRADITIONS ARE LIVING TRADITIONS

Another area that calls for some critical thinking is the fact that many Westerners present Asian spiritual traditions as having remained pristine and unchanging for thousands of years, but this is simply not true. As a professional historian, I study how Asian religions, healing systems, and martial arts are human constructs that have been built, propagated, and sustained by specific groups of people throughout history. Scholars like me often try to capture this perspective by saying that Asian traditions are "living traditions." This term is meant to emphasize the fact that traditions are constantly changing and never static. Spirituality is part of our ever-changing human culture and society, invariably undergoing tremendous shifts and transformations over time.

For an example of what I mean by a living tradition, think about how much the English language has changed over time. Have you ever read *Beowulf* in the original Old English? Written approximately a thousand years ago, it is completely illegible to a modern English-speaking reader. Have you read Shakespeare? That's only four hundred years old, but it is still very difficult to make sense of the language without proper training. It's not just language that has changed. Is there any aspect of our Western lives that is the same now as it was four hundred or a thousand years ago? Our food? Clothing? Art? Architecture? Medicine? Politics? Western religion hasn't stayed the same either, has it? There have been countless doctrinal developments, schisms, reforms, counter-reforms, and institutions that have been built and institutions that have collapsed over the centuries. It's important to realize that Asian culture is not any different.

The pace of this change has become even more pronounced in the modern period. In the last 150 years, all of the major Asian spiritual traditions have undergone radical restructuring in light of their encounters with modern technology. To illustrate what these changes can look like, I once spent a year and a half as a visiting scholar at a Buddhist temple outside of Taipei called Dharma Drum Mountain. This was a large monastic complex with lots of acreage, multiple ceremonial halls, and plenty of space for peaceful meditation. There also was a monastic college where monks and nuns studied Buddhist doctrine and learned to read Chinese Buddhist scriptures in a form of Chinese that is approximately 1,500 years old. But inside that college there also was a department dedicated to digitizing those same sutras. In that buzzing office, monastics and lay experts collaborated together to type the entire Buddhist textual canon into computers and then to digitally tag the text in XML markup language so that it could be keyword-searched by humans and analyzed by machines. The servers whirred and hummed, providing the world with access to this high-tech collection of scriptures, twenty-four hours a day, via the internet (if you're curious, you can visit the Chinese Buddhist Electronic Text Association at www.cbeta.org).

If that juxtaposition seems strange to you, you should know that, on the whole, Asian practitioners of all the traditions introduced in this book have embraced modern technology. They have increasingly utilized digital formats such as websites, podcasts, YouTube channels, and virtual collaboration platforms like WeChat and Zoom to share sacred knowledge. (In fact, all of this has become ubiquitous after the Covid-19 pandemic forced most people in Asia to limit their in-person interactions in the early 2020s.) Even more recently, I have seen AI chatbots that deliver the dharma online and robot priests conducting Buddhist services in Japan. And currently under development are wearable devices such as headsets that are designed to optimize one's meditation using brainwave biofeedback.

Another area where modernization has transformed spirituality is the relationship between spiritual and scientific worldviews. On the one hand, there are many proponents of Asian spiritual traditions who have argued that modern science is deficient or downright wrong and have instead doubled down on traditional ways of knowing. On the other hand, there are practitioners of Asian spiritual traditions of all kinds who have done the opposite and fully replaced traditional models with scientific ones. Finally, there are many proponents of Asian spirituality who see science and tradition as compatible or complementary in some way.

It's not important to me which one of the three positions you side with. In my view, the important thing is to be able to recognize the underlying assumptions behind people's arguments, which is a crucial part of thinking critically. We also don't need to simply accept someone's arguments about science—or any topic, really— just because they have had some spiritual realizations. Spiritual openings might give us a great deal of insight about the phenomenology of perception, the heart, and the energy body, but they don't necessarily give us any insight at all into scientific questions. (Just like you don't magically learn how to do math, speak French, or play the guitar from having spiritual experiences, either.)

In any case, as you set off on your spiritual explorations, be on the lookout for a common myth propagated by many groups that their specific way of doing things was founded thousands of years ago, and that this particular group has perfectly preserved the wisdom of their founder across the ages. Practitioners of such a tradition may wholeheartedly believe what they are saying, but they're just spouting marketing rhetoric. When we treat Asian traditions as living things rather than as static structures, we trade in the myth of a golden age for the reality of a constant flow of change. Instead of looking to the past for all the answers, we can appreciate how human ingenuity and creativity are always manifesting to reinterpret the past in the present day. And we can see our own contemporary spiritual explorations as part of that ongoing story.

From a historical perspective, there really is no such thing as a "pure" or "pristine" form of any living tradition. Every one of the Asian traditions I have discussed in this book has gone through constant change, transformation, and reinterpretation from the moment it was invented. There are often dozens or even hundreds of different interpretations of each doctrine or practice, which have continually changed depending on the time or place or context, and there's no one interpretation that is the "right one" to the exclusion of all others. To say that there is is just a form of fundamentalism.

ORIENTALISM AND CULTURAL APPROPRIATION

One of the reasons it is difficult for many Western explorers to think critically about Asian spiritual traditions or to see them as flawed, changing constructs is because of the prevalence of positive stereotypes about them. Scholars call the Western tendency to positively stereotype Asian things, and Asian spiritual traditions in particular, *Orientalism*. You won't find this term used much outside of scholarly discourses, but I think it's an essential addition to any spiritual explorer's critical-thinking toolbox.

A related term that you are probably already familiar with is *cultural appropriation*. This is the borrowing of symbols, practices, or other aspects of other cultures in a way that is inappropriate or ethically problematic. One especially reprehensible example is when companies use Asian spiritual symbols or words in order to sell unrelated stuff. I'm sure that you can think of multiple products and commodities being marketed in this way. Some examples that come to my own mind include a popular brand of popcorn that displays a big pink cartoon of the Buddha prominently on the bag and a popular brand of tea that features photos of meditating women against a background of Indian henna designs.

These companies are betting that we consumers will associate these images—as well as words like *Zen*, *Buddha*, or *yogi*, which they use in their brand names and slogans—with desirable attributes like relaxation and well-being. In essence, cultural appropriation works as an advertising strategy because mainstream Western consumers already have internalized Orientalist biases that associate Asian spiritual symbols with positive feelings. The two things are closely intertwined together and feed off one another.

If images and terminology from Asian spiritual traditions influence our choice of popcorn or tea, how much more will the same tactics influence us when it comes to our choices in the spiritual marketplace? In fact, Western spiritual seekers are very likely to become entranced by Orientalism when it comes time to choosing spiritual teachers, workshops, books, and related merchandise, allowing positive stereotypes to cloud their judgment.

One of my favorite movies related to Asian spiritual traditions, the 2011 film *Kumaré*, directed by the Indian American filmmaker Vikram Gandhi, dives deeply into this topic. In this exposé of Americans' Orientalist attitudes toward Asian spiritual traditions, the filmmaker dons Hindu robes and beads, imitates a strong Indian accent, and pretends to be a guru recently arrived in the US. He starts leading bogus workshops where he teaches gibberish mantras, invented meditations, and rituals that are completely meaningless. Soon enough, he gathers around him a group of gullible devotees who are hanging on his every word and worshipping the ground he walks on.

I won't give away what happens when, at the end of the film, Gandhi reveals to his followers that he's been lying to them all along. (Though I will note that their reactions are priceless.) For our purposes here, it is enough for me to point out that the Orientalism of the spiritual seekers in the film is the main reason that Gandhi could so easily pull off this scam. It is also one of the main reasons that it is so easy for Asian gurus and charismatic teachers to dupe people into following them even when they are clearly engaging in sexual misconduct, financial shenanigans, and other unethical behavior. The positive stereotypes of Orientalism act as blinders, influencing people to overlook red flags in spiritual circles that they would definitely think twice about if they were in any other context.

You might be thinking to yourself, is it even possible when you live in a culture that's so riddled with Orientalism to ethically engage in Asian spiritual traditions in a way that avoids cultural appropriation? This is a highly personal question that requires each individual to examine their own actions and motives with clarity and honesty. I'll give you my own thoughts here, but please do your own critical thinking and determine for yourself where you stand on this.

To me, engaging ethically with knowledge that comes from another culture ultimately comes down to being aware of and respectful of the power dynamics. With Asian traditions in particular, I think it's essential to bear in mind that between the sixteenth and twentieth centuries, Western powers invaded or attacked every country in Asia. With few exceptions, those countries were forcibly taken over, subjected to Western rule, and exploited for financial profit. As part of their efforts to exert control over their colonies, European authorities racialized and subjugated Asian people and denigrated their indigenous cultures and traditions. Religious institutions were dismantled and even outlawed. Sacred relics and other cultural treasures were pillaged and transported to European and American museums and art dealerships. This massive cultural genocide and theft is still an open wound that has not been resolved or repaired (and it is rarely acknowledged or even heard of among Western spiritual seekers).

Given that history, it's necessary for us to constantly question the power dynamics at play when we engage with any kind of cultural heritage that we were not born into. It is important to ensure that we are approaching our studies of Asian spiritual traditions with humility—less like consumers with demands and opinions, and more like guests who are willing to learn, engage, and be challenged. We must remain constantly on guard against overstepping, disrespecting, taking for granted, or misunderstanding the traditions we're learning.

At the same time we maintain that kind of humility and respect, we can also plainly recognize that many Asian spiritual traditions characterize themselves as universally applicable teachings that are recommended to help anyone and everyone regardless of their background. Buddhism, for example, was spread across Asia and eventually around the world by missionary monks whose goal was to share the dharma with as many people as possible globally. According to the stories, the Buddha himself mandated that his followers spread his teaching widely in whatever languages or cultural contexts were necessary to reach the masses. Committed Buddhists commonly believe that introducing new people to even a small amount of Buddhist practice is a beneficial "Dharma Gate" that can lessen their suffering and lead to their eventual liberation.

Each has its own particular history, but there are similar stories behind the international spread of most forms of yoga, Advaita, Chinese cultural practices like martial arts and medicine, and other Asian spiritual traditions. None of the bodies of knowledge or practices I've written about in this book were stolen by Westerners from a group of unwilling indigenous people. In all cases, these traditions and techniques were brought to the West or taught to Western adherents by Asian teachers, gurus, or masters who believed these practices should be spread beyond the borders of the original culture in which they developed. Today, centuries after those initial cross-cultural contacts, Asian spiritual knowledge flows freely across our globalized and digitally connected world. There are hundreds of millions of webpages and thousands upon thousands of books and workshops teaching these traditions in English.

For all of these reasons, it's hard to make a blanket accusation that someone who is earnestly engaging with Asian spiritual traditions is committing cultural appropriation. Furthermore, to turn our backs on the benefits that could be gained from this plethora of knowledge because of a fear of cultural appropriation would be shortsighted.

BOX 8.1: Self-Reflection on Orientalism
and Cultural Appropriation

Here are some questions that will serve you well as you reflect on how to engage with Asian spiritual traditions in an ethical and non-extractive kind of way. It may be helpful to actually write out your answers, as this promotes clearer thinking than just mulling something over in your head.

1. Am I clear about my motivations for learning this tradition? Am I truly interested in how this practice will benefit my own life and development, or do I have ulterior motives such as fitting in with a particular social group or playing out a certain identity in front of my peers?
2. Am I freely being invited to learn this teaching by the teachers or lineage holders of this knowledge? Am I aware of the power dynamics in my relationship with them? Is this tradition freely offering this knowledge to me, or am I engaged in some kind of manipulation or power play in order to gain access to it?
3. Am I giving credit back to the source of the tradition? Am I cultivating gratitude for the originators of this tradition and the line of teachers who brought me this opportunity to learn? Are there ways that I can demonstrate my thanks, support, or otherwise honor the culture and context that gave birth to this spiritual tradition?
4. Am I aware of and am I respecting this group's history? Am I respecting the cultural conventions of the originators of this tradition? Am I learning how to properly navigate this social context with respect?
5. Am I absolutely sure I am understanding this teaching correctly? Am I going the extra mile in order to make sure that I am informed and knowledgeable about this tradition's terminology, symbolism, doctrines, philosophies, etc.? How would I know if I was misunderstanding, misrepresenting, or reinventing this information?

On the other hand, I hope you'll agree that there is a clear ethical difference between earnest engagement and mere commercial consumption. For example, if you're wearing Hindu mala beads and sporting an OM T-shirt as a fashion statement, but you're not really aware of the traditional meanings or uses of these symbols, then you might want to check yourself. If you're really making an authentic effort to learn about a particular Hindu tradition as part of your spiritual path and not just engaging in spiritual materialism, then you'll likely be more focused on your own development rather than what products you're buying.

Ultimately, only you can truly understand your reasons for the decisions you make, and only you can ensure that your spiritual path is grounded in an ethical approach. It is imperative to interrogate yourself and be honest with what you find. This kind of critical thinking is not optional or superfluous but rather is itself an integral part of your journey of self-reflection and deepening self-discovery.

AVOIDING LAZY AND CONFUSING CONFLATIONS

One of the best ways to ensure that we are not engaging in cultural appropriation is to move past superficial understandings and to make sincere efforts to understand deeply the traditions we are learning. This involves learning to engage with Asian traditions on their own terms. One of the most basic starting points is making sure to avoid conflating traditions together. By conflation, I mean an oversimplified comparison that explains one thing by simply asserting it's the same as something else.

In chapter 1, I critiqued one common kind of conflation: the notion that all Asian spiritual traditions are just "different roads leading up the same mountain." Now that you've read the rest of the book, you might agree with me that this view is misinformed and drastically oversimplified. You've hopefully by now come to appreciate how different Buddhism, Hinduism, and Chinese traditions are from one another, as well as how much internal diversity there is within each of these broad categories, even when it comes to the most basic ideas and practices.

Aside from conflating different forms of Asian spiritual traditions with one another, people frequently conflate Asian spiritual traditions with Western bodies of knowledge too. This is just as lazy and just as confusing. Consider these statements:

The Buddha's teachings on compassion are pretty much the same as the teachings of Jesus.

Advaita's notion of the Self is essentially the same as quantum physics.

The model of the mind that's found in yogic meditation is basically the same as in Western psychology.

All of these statements are conflations because they seek to explain the unique contributions of Asian spiritual traditions by making an oversimplified comparison to something Western. That's not to say there are *no* similarities between the things being compared in the statements above. But ask yourself: Is that really the most accurate way to describe them? Is it the most respectful way? Do we always need to use Western or modern concepts as the yardsticks we're measuring against?

Let me make an analogy to food. It's not like there are *no* similarities between Chinese dumplings and Italian raviolis. Indeed, you might even find that it's helpful to explain what a Chinese dumpling is to someone that never has seen one by saying "it's like a ravioli." But that certainly is just a starting point, not the whole story. It may quickly get a preliminary picture into the person's head, but you need to immediately start to complicate that picture. "It's like a ravioli but folded differently so as to make a crescent-like shape," you might say. "And the filling is made of pork, cabbage, scallions, garlic, and ginger instead of cheese. And they can be steamed or fried in addition to being boiled. And you dip them in a combination of soy sauce and vinegar. And they are commonly handmade by Chinese families during the Lunar New Year season." So forth and so on.

In just such a way, you might choose to give a complete novice to Asian spirituality a starting point by saying that there are some similarities between Buddhist teachings and Christianity, psychology, or quantum physics. But if you choose to use that kind of comparison as a convenient place to begin, you should then swiftly move on to pointing out all the differences and divergences.

We spiritual explorers of Asian spirituality all need to reflect critically on how well we are representing these traditions when we talk with others in order to make sure we are doing so clearly and accurately. This can also help us determine how well we understand the nuances of these traditions ourselves. Perhaps one reason that Westerners are constantly conflating Asian spiritual systems is that we don't actually understand them that well ourselves. Making loose parallels might just be a way of glossing over the fact that we don't have clarity about some of the specifics.

In the interests of helping you diagnose where you might be a bit weak in your own understanding of the Asian spiritual traditions I've discussed in this book, I've provided some review questions in box 8.2 that focus on disentangling some common conflations. I invite you to take some time and honestly reflect on each one. Where are the weak points in your comprehension? Are there sections of this book you need to go back and reread? Are there external resources that you need to track down to deepen your understanding? How can you best support your ongoing learning and exploration of these topics?

LOST IN TRANSLATION

If we're going to do a deep dive into Asian spiritual traditions and really try to understand them on their own terms, sooner or later we're going to run up against the issue of translation. This can be an immensely challenging area for Western spiritual explorers to navigate, one that requires sharp critical-thinking skills.

The underlying obstacle, of course, is that the typical Western explorer does not know any Asian languages. Western yogis rarely learn to read Sanskrit, Western Zen meditators rarely learn to read classical Chinese or Japanese, Western Tibetan Buddhists rarely learn to read or speak Tibetan, and so forth. (In fact, I'm appalled at how many Western spiritual teachers don't even know how to properly pronounce the basic keywords of the Asian traditions

BOX 8.2: Self-Assessment on
Key Asian Spiritual Concepts

Uh-oh, it's a pop quiz from the professor! Here are some questions to help you reflect on the finer distinctions between Asian spiritual traditions, in order to help you
determine where you might need to gain more clarity and a deeper understanding. It
may be helpful to actually write out your answers, as this promotes clearer thinking
than just mulling something over in your head. Also, try to answer the questions
in your own words, so you can test if you are drawing on your own knowledge or
simply regurgitating what I said.

1. What are some of the major ways that the practice of yoga has changed
   from the ancient period to the present?
2. What are some of the main differences between the major schools
   of Buddhism?
3. How are basic Chinese spiritual principles different from Indian ones?
4. What are some of the major differences between the Western engagement with Asian spiritual traditions in the past versus the present?
5. What is the distinction between neo-Advaita's version of nonduality
   and Buddhism's?
6. How do practices for nondual perception, heart, and energy represent
   different orientations to spiritual growth?
7. What are some major differences between Theravada, Mahayana,
   Vajrayana, Advaita, Tantric, and Taoist notions of enlightenment?
8. What is the difference between spiritual materialism and spiritual
   bypassing?
9. What is the difference between Orientalism and cultural appropriation?
10. What are some of the advantages gained by approaching Asian tradi-
    tions critically?

they claim to be experts in!) While it's perhaps understandable
that most people don't have the time and energy to dedicate years
to acquiring these skills, spiritual explorers who can't access the
original languages find themselves in the difficult position of never

being a hundred percent sure about what their favorite traditions are actually saying.

I underwent years of language training in graduate school, and I have a lot of experience translating Chinese Buddhist texts into English. I have published these translations, have led teams of scholars in major translation projects, and have also taught graduate-level seminars on translation. So, this is an area in which I have an extensive background. One of my favorite examples to use with my students to illustrate the need for critical thinking about translation is the first two lines of the classic text the *Tao Te Ching*, by Lao Tzu (see more information about this text and a translation of the full chapter in chapter 2).

In my view, the first chapter of the *Tao Te Ching* is one of the most eloquent expressions of nonduality ever written. Without question, it is also one of the most influential statements in Asian spiritual literature. The opening lines are extremely well known to most Chinese-speaking people, perhaps of equal stature to Shakespeare's famous "To be or not to be" quote for English speakers.

The *Tao Te Ching* has been translated many times into English, so there have been many different ways that these opening lines have been rendered. The original in Chinese is a twelve-character phrase that reads:

道可道非常道；名可名非常名。
Dao ke dao fei chang dao; ming ke ming fei chang ming.

There is a basic pattern going on here that is easy to understand grammatically: "The x that can be x'ed is not the eternal x," repeated two times. The first time through, *x* is the word *dao*, meaning the *Tao* or the nondual totality of the cosmos. The second time through, *x* is the word *ming*, a basic Chinese term that means to give something a name or to identify it.

With this information in hand, let's see what some English translators have done with these lines, shall we? One of the earliest, James Legge, translated those lines in 1891 as follows:

The Tao that can be trodden is not the enduring and unchanging Tao.
The name that can be named is not the enduring and unchanging name.

Shortly thereafter, in 1895, another early translator, G. G. Alexander, treated the lines in this way:

God (the great everlasting infinite First Cause from whom all things
in heaven and earth proceed) can neither be defined nor named.

Wait, huh? What a huge difference! What's going on here? Well, let's take out our critical thinking magnifying glass and take a closer look.

Upon examining these two translations, the first thing we can notice is that Legge's translation repeats the basic pattern twice ("the x that can be x'ed is not the eternal x"), following the original Chinese word order closely. Alexander, on the other hand, departs from the Chinese pattern completely. He condenses the two lines into a single quick statement that "God can neither be defined nor named," and inserts a long parenthetical explanation of what he means by "God" that is found nowhere in the original text.

An important second distinction to notice is that Legge approached his translation in a way that emphasized the Taoist origin of the original text. Two out of the three times "Tao" appears, he chose not to translate the word, leaving it in Chinese as a signal to the reader that it's a specialized term. Alexander, on the other hand, chose to replace "Tao" with the English term "God." I'm sure he meant well, thinking that this would improve the ability of his nineteenth-century readers to understand what the passage means, but talk about conflation!

Other translators coming later used a panoply of other words to translate "Tao" in their renditions of these same lines, including "Providence" (E. H. Parker, 1903) and "Reason" (D. T. Suzuki and Paul Carus, 1913). Not only did these translators use divergent translation terms for Tao; they also chose to capture the overall meaning of the opening lines in different ways.

I'm going through this example at this level of detail so you can appreciate exactly why I think Legge's translation is a pretty good one. Legge attempts to preserve the original Chinese structure and uses more precise translation terminology. Alexander's, on the other hand, is a terrible translation. He completely ignores the Chinese word order and inserts Western terms and long phrases that are not in the original text. I think you would agree that if you wanted to read the *Tao Te Ching* to learn about Taoist views of nonduality, you would be much better served by reading Legge than by reading Alexander.

And herein lies the problem: Which of these two translations is better might be obvious to you now, but how could you possibly have known any of that if I hadn't just walked you through it? How can you evaluate the quality of a translation when you don't read the original language? Unfortunately, I don't think there is much you can do. If you don't read the original language, you have no idea if a translator is being accurate in their choice of words or being faithful to the structure of the text. You have no idea if the translator is inserting their own interpretations, making unwarranted connections or leaps, or using misleading terminology. In fact, you can't even tell the difference between a competent translator and someone who is completely making it up as they go along!

Just in case you're thinking that people can't possibly publish made-up translations, you should know that a great number of published translations of the Chinese *Tao Te Ching* and *I-Ching*, the Hindu *Bhagavad Gita*, the Buddhist *Dharmapada*, and many other major Asian spiritual classics have been authored by people who can't even read the original languages. They are simply "reinterpreting" translations done by more competent people who came before them. (On a related note, you should also know that all of those lovely Rumi quotes that circulate online are also reinterpretations rather that translations, and nearly all of the Buddha quotes going around social media are completely fabricated!)

There are some steps you can take to try to improve the quality of information you are receiving. You can, for example, take the time to evaluate translators' credentials. When it comes to historical texts, I would recommend translations done by academic authors rather than religious figures, since I believe they tend to make more of an effort to be neutral and accurate. (In the resources mentioned at the end of chapter 2, I recommended the translations in the Norton Anthology of World Religions series as a great starting point.)

If you think critically about it further, you'll see that all of my comments here about written translations equally apply to oral teachings. If you don't understand the original, how can you tell what liberties are being taken with the meaning of what's being said?

In general, whatever spiritual tradition you are into, it is important to constantly think critically about the accuracy of the information you are being given. The better your information, the better you'll be able to avoid making unintentional conflations. The better you'll be able to understand Asian spirituality on its own terms. The better you'll be able to appreciate the nuances of the different teachings.

As for me, whenever I am encountering for the first time a teaching that comes from a language I do not read, I put on my critical-thinking cap right away. I never take what I am reading or being told as infallible, and I always ask myself what is potentially being lost in translation. Keeping such questions in your mind too will hopefully help you maintain a healthy skepticism toward any one person's interpretation of Asian spiritual teachings and continually hone your judgment and discernment. Most of all, it should encourage you to keep learning as much as you can about the traditions you care about. Ensuring you are knowledgeable and savvy about the information you are receiving is going to take some legwork on your part. Take it from me—it can easily become a lifelong study, if you're serious about it!

(By the way, of all the options, my opinion is that the best translation of the *Tao Te Ching* is the one freely available online by the scholar A. C. Muller, which I quoted in chapter 2. Flip to page 46 to see how he rendered those famous first two lines.)

—————————

This chapter has explored some critical perspectives that will help you quite a bit in your further explorations of the Asian spiritual territory. These have included a number of ways to be judicious about the information you are consuming and to reflect on your own biases and potential misunderstandings. There are many other critical perspectives we haven't been able to explore here, but some additional considerations are broached in the resources recommended in box 8.3.

Over the years, I've heard many Western spiritual practitioners demonize analytical thought, speaking as if thought is the mortal enemy of spirituality, but I couldn't disagree more! To be sure, being "lost in thought" and unable to break out of a wild ride your discursive mind has taken you on is a major impediment to spiritual practice for many people. I can sympathize. As an academic who uses my thinking brain all day long to do my job, I used to find it quite difficult to turn it off long enough to sink into a state of relaxation or peace. However, let's not swing the pendulum all the way over to the other extreme.

In my opinion, our powers to think carefully and use discernment are centrally important parts of the spiritual path. For all the reasons I've laid out in this chapter, if critical thinking is not part of the toolkit you bring with you on your spiritual exploration, it's very likely that you will get tangled up in some avoidable obstacles and will go down some blind alleys on your way to growth and self-discovery. It's very likely that you will be projecting your own biases, ideals, or fantasies onto Asian traditions rather than authentically engaging with them on their own terms.

To me, the thinking mind is a natural part of our humanity and an important asset that can and should be integrated into our spiritual lives. That means leaning into analysis and reflection—not allowing it to dominate our lives at the expense of everything else but making sure that we carefully consider the things we care about from as many different angles as possible.

BOX 8.3: Additional Resources Related to
Critical Perspectives in This Chapter

MEDIA

- *Black Beryl Podcast*—This is my own podcast, dedicated to the intersection of Buddhism, Asian medicine, and embodied spirituality. Interviewees include both scholars and practitioners, and most prioritize critical perspectives.
- *Kumaré*—Did I mention how much I like this film? Don't miss it!

BOOKS

- Wakoh Shannon Hickey, *Mind Cure: How Meditation Became Medicine*— Revealing the diverse history of yoga and meditation in America, along with a valuable social critique of the contemporary mindfulness movement
- Jane Iwamura, *Virtual Orientalism: Asian Religions and American Popular Culture*—A great primer on Orientalism related to Asian spiritual traditions
- Andrea Jain, *Selling Yoga: From Counterculture to Pop Culture*—A critique of how yoga has been popularized and commercialized in the modern West
- Pierce Salguero, *Buddhish: A Guide to the Twenty Most Important Buddhist Ideas for the Curious and Skeptical*—An introduction to Buddhism that shares a number of critical perspectives about different aspects of this tradition

This kind of critical thinking is not something you can just do once and be done with it. As you proceed on your spiritual journey, it's vitally important to continually reflect at each step. For me, I would unequivocally say that critical thinking has been an integral part of my own spiritual practice. As with all practices, it's something that maybe feels awkward at first, but you get better at it with time. You can be confident that over the long run it will reward you with more and more opportunities for growth and discovery as you continue to explore.

POSTSCRIPT

We started this journey eight chapters ago with a plan to cut through the noise and for me to provide you with a clear road map for the exploration of Asian spiritual traditions. I asked you to place your trust in me and promised that I would give you an honest, balanced, and thoughtful tour of the spiritual territory. I told you that I would approach this material from my own perspective as a long-time scholar and practitioner of these methods, but that I would always encourage you to be "a lamp unto yourself"—meaning to make your own decisions about what is right for you. I hope you feel I have lived up to these promises.

Now that we have arrived at the end of the book, I wish to thank you for joining me on this excursion. It has been a real privilege to be your guide.

Really, though, the journey has just begun, hasn't it? As the philosopher Alfred Korzybski famously put it, "The map is not the territory." After all, this book is just a map pointing out the features of the landscape and indicating some of the well-trodden paths that crisscross the land. How you use this map and where you go next is completely up to you.

As you set out on your journey, I want to remind you that although you might wish to carry this map with you for now, never forget that you are the leader of your own expedition. Remember to listen to your own inner guidance (or your inner light, or your inner zebra—pick your metaphor!) more than to any of the words I've written. Eventually, when you no longer need this map, feel free to discard it. Like the backwoods hiker who has learned every contour of the hills, once you're familiar with the territory, you'll be able to direct yourself wherever you want to go and to guide others without needing to refer back to any map at all.

So, all of that being said, let me wish you goodbye for now. Wherever you are headed, wherever your travels take you, I wish you happy trails. I truly hope that you find the destination that you are looking for. Or, perhaps, that you eventually come to realize that there is no destination other than the journey itself. It is also my hope that someday, perhaps a long time into the future, you may remember to return back home and share with us where you've been and what you've learned.

Now, take up your lamp, fellow explorer, and set off on your adventure!

ACKNOWLEDGMENTS

This book is the product of a lifetime of engagement with Asian spiritual traditions, during which time I have learned from countless people. I am grateful for every teacher, every encounter, every conversation along the way. As the manuscript was coming together, I got feedback on drafts from Misha BearWoman Metzler, Lorena Ribeiro, Amy Caldwell, Gary Falk, Jack Morrigan, June Newman, Jeff Richards, Mike Salguero, and Michael Stanley-Baker. I am grateful to all of them for sharing their reactions and suggestions.